W0227947

DARING TO DREAM

In the depths of your hopes and desires
lies your silent knowledge of the beyond,
And like seeds dreaming beneath the snow,
Your heart dreams of spring
Trust the dreams for in them is
hidden the gate to eternity.

–Kahlil Gibran, *The Prophet*

DARING TO DREAM

Cultivating Corporate Creativity Through Dreamwork

ANJALI HAZARIKA

www.sagepublications.com

Los Angeles • London • New Delhi • Singapore • Washington DC • Boston

Copyright © Anjali Hazarika, 1997

All rights reserved. No part of this book may be reproduced or utilized in any form or by any means, electronic or mechanical, including photocopying, recording or by any information storage or retrieval system, without permission in writing from the publisher.

First published in 1997 by

SAGE Response
B1/I-1 Mohan Cooperative Industrial Area
Mathura Road, New Delhi 110 044, India

SAGE Publications Inc
2455 Teller Road
Thousand Oaks, California 91320, USA

SAGE Publications Ltd
1 Oliver's Yard, 55 City Road
London EC1Y 1SP, United Kingdom

SAGE Publications Asia-Pacific Pte Ltd
3 Church Street
#10-04 Samsung Hub
Singapore 049483

Published by Vivek Mehra for SAGE Publications India Pvt Ltd, lasertypeset by Innovative Processors, 4819/24 Ansari Road, New Delhi and printed at Saurabh Printers Pvt Ltd, New Delhi.

Fourth Printing 2015

Library of Congress Cataloging-in-Publication Data

Hazarika, Anjali.
      Daring to dream: cultivating corporate creativity through dreamwork/Anjali Hazarika.
            p. cm.   (c: alk. paper)   (pbk.: alk. paper)
      Includes bibliographical references and index.
      1. Creative ability in business. 2. Dreams. I. Title.
      HD53.H39   650 1—dc21   1997   97-31051

ISBN: 10: 0-8039-9397-8 (US-HB)   10: 81-7036-650-X (India-HB)
          13: 978-0-8039-9397-6 (US-HB)   13: 978-81-7036-650-8 (India-HB)
          10: 0-8039-9398-6 (US-PB)   10: 81-7036-651-8 (India-PB)
          13: 978-0-8039-9398-3 (US-PB)   13: 978-81-7036-651-5 (India-PB)

The SAGE Team: Shyama Warner, Jaya Chowdhury and Santosh Rawat

Thank you Baba
for holding my hand
so that I could walk in the light of your faith in me

Foreword

WE ARE BLESSED with two naturally recurring states of consciousness. One, our waking consciousness, is devoted to the task of finding our way in what is more and more of a man-made world. The other, our dreaming consciousness, has an inward focus assessing to what extent what we are doing 'out there' meets two basic human needs, namely, to give and receive love (and thus preserve our connectedness to others) and our freedom (to be all that we can be in a way that is congruent with the first need). The problem, of course, is that our remarkable achievements awake have come about at a terrible cost to our stature as human beings, creating a level of suffering and a degree of moral slippage that seems to be increasing daily. In our concern with waking accomplishments we have failed to give due concern to the innate repair mechanisms available to us nightly in the dreams we dream. What are these repair mechanisms? They are none other than the basic phenomenological features of dream imagery. Our dreams focus on the needs and concerns that are arising at the moment as we move into the future. They shed light on aspects of our past that emotionally connect to these concerns and reflect back to us truths about ourselves that elude us while awake.

In a unique undertaking, Dr Anjali Hazarika has set out to restore the balance between problematic aspects of waking life and this readily available repair mechanism. With some measure of trepidation and a good deal of courage, she has taken upon herself the task of testing the usefulness of dreamwork in what one might not expect to be a very receptive area—the practical world of business. She has met with remarkable success. The book is the story of her commitment to this task. There are three reasons for her success.

Globalization of the economy is bringing to the fore issues of transformation and change. Expansion of the bureaucratic structure and entrenched ways of doing things, effective in the past, are not apt to provide the level of flexibility, 'intelligent risk-taking' and the release of the degree of creative energy needed to meet the challenge. Corporate structures, as currently organized, fall far short of providing a milieu favourable to liberating such energies at every level of the organization.

The second reason for the author's success is her recognition of the timely need to explore the personal subjective fallout in the lives of those who are so intimately involved in the corporate structure. The level of competition and the curtailment of personal recognition and involvement make for a degree of alienation that undermines morale and limits creative output. It is into this terrain that she has driven a beachhead through her skill in working with dreams. The presentation of her work is enriched by an extended account of what is known about creativity in general, and more specifically of the intrinsic link between dreams and creativity. This aspect of dreaming, often appreciated by writers and occasionally by scientists, has never been given its just due.

The third reason is the author herself, the passion and dedication she has brought to the task, her mastery of the ins and outs of the business world and most of all her natural intelligence about the nature of dreams.

Her experience, now ensconced in various segments of the petroleum industry in India over the past decade, speaks to the way these special features of the dream have a place in the fostering of both organizational and personal change. Dreamwork is unique among personnel development techniques in the depth to which it probes the subjective cost of fitting into corporate structures as they now exist. Dr Hazarika has focused on managers, working with them both in groups and individually, although organizational change is the ultimate goal. Such change begins with changes in the managers themselves through the dreamwork. They are the ones who can see to it that whatever change is necessary percolates throughout the entire system. In the author's own words, dreamwork can 'fast-forward' both organizational and personal change.

There is another interesting feature to dreamwork that Dr Hazarika does not explicitly mention but that implicitly flows from the way she conducts her groups. The process itself reflects the organizational goals being sought. The work proceeds in a flat rather than a hierarchical structure. Each person who shares a dream is the ultimate expert on that dream. Everyone participates in the goal of helping the dreamer. There is no private or hidden agenda. All become helpers to the dreamer and benefit from the satisfaction derived from that role. A sense of interconnectedness and communion pervades the work. For the desired endpoint to be reached, a certain degree of risk-taking is involved on the part of the dreamer. He or she must have the courage to challenge a given status quo. Substitute the dreamer for the corporation, the managers for the group, and the dream for problematic issues, and you have a model in which all parties concerned benefit. In the process of realizing at a microscopic level (the dream group), the idealized macroscopic (organization) goals come into focus.

In our near-total focus on waking consciousness, we have left our dreams behind. By and large they are only of passing concern, piquing our curiosity for the moment and of serious concern only to psychoanalysts. We are, in effect, a dream-deprived society. Over the past two decades there have been some efforts to remedy this and to move dreamwork beyond the consulting room. In this respect Dr Hazarika's contribution is of signal importance. If dreams can be introduced into the business industry, and her work is a clear indication that a beginning has been made, there remains the hope that it can ultimately find its proper niche in all sectors of society.

Written in a very personal style, Dr Hazarika's book is infused with a lively sense of metaphor, as well as illustrative parables and quotes from the folklore and literature of India. All in all, a delight to read and much to ponder over.

Montague Ullman, M.D.
Ardsley, New York

Contents

ONE

Introduction: Discovering a Dream

A DECADE AGO I found myself at a crossroads, faced with a difficult choice. Should I cross the traditional boundary in management education and venture into the entirely different and somewhat esoteric world of dreams? Or should I continue to work with the familiar?

The first option would involve the use of dreamwork as an alternative model for stimulating creativity in business. It would be radically different from the existing stereotype, which emphasizes improving current practices and profits by going further along a well-plotted path.

There would be no plotted path with dreamwork. I would have to be prepared to venture into unknown territories. I might have to sacrifice the security of a safe approach in which one can count on arriving at a predictable goal. I would need to take risks and give up cherished methods and beliefs. I might even encounter periods of deep uncertainty and frustration, when it would seem that my efforts were leading nowhere. And I would need to do all this to find new approaches for solving real problems in the real world. But in the process, it might allow me to gain the confidence, ability and authority to interpret my own experiences as reflected in dreams.

A dream is not just a dream, it is an invocation to develop greater awareness. It is an ocean of possibilities, a blueprint of an attainable reality. A dream presents an opportunity for exploring and identifying those possibilities that enhance the capacity to envision and create the future. It is a dream both in the sense of being within reach and in the sense of being a long way away from current reality. It has the potential to create a future that may not exist without the dream. And if it is a 'big dream' such as that of a Gandhi or a Martin Luther King, it can become the source of inspiration to many.

Translating that dream into reality in order to provide guidance through uncharted territories and continuously changing times is very important. Moving from dreaming to doing requires an openness to learn, and the ability to envision and understand change, and innovate and act effectively in completely new situations. This is one ability that separates average managers from those that excel. While the former react to a predictable future, the latter are able to shape a qualitatively new one. Walking along this unplotted path, my instinct told me, would be full of adventure and daring, and perhaps would even be fulfilling.

And so I took the critical decision of embarking upon this exciting journey along an unplotted path.

For the past several years I have been developing and conducting creativity and dream workshops for corporate executives from diverse sectors of business. The basic objective has been to introduce a holistic model of stimulating creativity through dreamwork. What began as mere exploration gradually transformed itself into the quest of a lifetime. It was not enough just to tell people about this new insight—it was important that they experienced it in a way that evoked its full power and potential.

My doctoral work developed and redefined dreamwork as a new paradigm for management development and established it as a nexus to creativity. Working on the dissertation was like a joyride largely because working on dreams in itself is great fun.

It is a way of leading a fuller life because it brings our thoughts, emotions and experiences all on one plane.

The idea for this book was triggered by my interaction with the participants at my workshops. Several of them expressed an interest to identify and learn specific skills that could enhance creativity. This book is a response to their demand. Through this book I am also sharing my joy and excitement in working on dreams. I hope my enthusiasm will touch the hearts and minds of a few and get more and more people interested in dreamwork.

From dreaming to doing

The title and the principal metaphor of this book comes from my belief in the practical utility of dream workshops. It also stems from the daring and courage to offer creativity and dream workshops in organizations where creativity is valued but techniques to enhance alternative models of creativity are frequently ignored. Even within the range of techniques that can be considered, why would anyone have wanted to adopt a soft, subjective approach such as dreaming for seeking hard, objective solutions to business problems? It was like introducing the feminine, the intuitive and the subjective elements into what is widely regarded as the masculine, the rational, the objective and somewhat mechanistic pattern of managerial thinking. For long, the corporate world has been part of the public, conscious domain, whereas dreaming so clearly belongs to the private, unconscious domain. It requires an unusual combination of risk-taking and daring to integrate these opposites to challenge the basic tenets of traditional management education.

The credit for this path-breaking work goes to Dr Francis Menezes, Director of the Tata Management Training Centre, Pune, and founder President of the Indian Association for the Study of Dreams, who introduced dreamwork into management education in India in the mid-1980s. It was also he who subsequently initiated me into dreamwork.

At that time, I was becoming increasingly frustrated with the traditional methods of management education. While they had their uses, I felt that there was a crying need for newer methods to foster creative abilities in an environment defined by continual change. If the creative process is a process of change—of development and of evolution—then a fresh, transcendental approach was required that in itself had the potential to create new conditions.

This does not mean that the past does not hold any lessons. But like a trail through a forest, which becomes more and more faint and finally seems to disappear, the value of traditional management education, too, quickly diminishes for the creative, the gifted, the intuitive manager. It is silent about 'spirituality in business' and ways to rekindle the spirit in work. It does not concern itself with the dynamics of integrating intellect, intuition and the subconscious, all of which can produce remarkable answers and practical solutions to one's deepest concerns at work. As the 'business of business' is becoming more demanding, this sense of purpose and contribution is being increasingly lost. Willis Harman, former President of the Institute of Neotic Sciences, USA, reminds us that we seem to be ignoring the fact that business is actually meant to provide nourishment and life to society, as the Swedish word *'narings liv'* means in that language. This is what has inspired me to work on stimulating creativity through dreams.

Everyone has creative potential of some kind and in some degree. For instance, have we not all experienced that 'exciting moment' when we do something in a way that has not been simply handed over to us but is of our own making? However, creativity gets thwarted in the process of growing up, and for a variety of reasons we do not believe in it. This prevents us from exploring the outer limits of our selves. Our conditioning does not permit us to break the boundaries between the known self and the evolving self, between the rational self and the intuitive self, between the dreaming self and the waking self. As a result, we deprive ourselves of insights that would have enriched us with dreams and images from deeper states of consciousness. Although we sometimes realize their immense value, our general tendency is to not talk about such 'inner moments of truth' unless we find ourselves in a safe setting and among like-minded people where this kind of sharing is possible without guilt, fear or shame.

Dream groups often provide this kind of setting within organizations. The work I have done with several hundred managers (a large majority of whom were men) confirms that the process of dreamwork often succeeds in forming a creative mind-set that is sensitive to gaps, missing elements and disharmonies related to the problem at hand, and receptive to unconventional thoughts. It fosters the ability to see things in unusual ways, to make meaningful, new connections between past experiences and present associations by bringing them into a common pool, and to integrate new perspectives.

It emphasizes such things as deliberate metaphorical thinking, tolerance of ambiguity and complexity, exploration of a large number of alternatives, and systematic analysis of the requirements of a problem situation. These penetrate deep into the course of thought, redirecting the pattern of thinking itself. From the organizational point of view, the workshops often succeed in exploding the common myth that creativity is the preserve of only the gifted few.

The critical business issues that we face today all relate to change—from downsizing and right sizing to re-engineering and restructuring. Thus, in this regard, the most critical issues are *awareness* and *consciousness,* since nothing can change without a changed perception of reality. And everything begins to change in the right direction as soon as there is a changed perception of reality. Awareness is not only crucial but has to be systematically cultivated and also properly institutionalized. Lack of awareness of change will not allow new inputs to penetrate into corporate strategy. For example, information technology can provide diverse inputs and facilitate continuous knowledge sharing. But this may not be realized without proper awareness. Thus, awareness is as crucial to creativity as creativity is to business survival.

The power of dreamwork is such that it makes the dreamer aware of a whole new territory of mental space, much larger and more complex than the one explored during the waking state. It enhances awareness about all that goes on around us. This awareness gives us the ability to respond, to make numerous choices every day, to improve our performance, to strategize against competitors, to seize opportunities to accomplish our goals, to win customers. Creativity in its simplest form is the ability to choose from myriads of possibilities of thought, feeling and action in order to respond meaningfully to the moment.

From dreaming to daring

As you might imagine, this book, which marks a departure from traditional ways of harnessing corporate creativity, could not have been conceivable in the pre-globalization era. The subsequent seven chapters of the book are designed to enhance corporate as well as individual creativity. While readers may perceive a sexist bias in these chapters, it is not intentional—the male gender has been used only to avoid awkwardness of expression.

The second chapter, 'Creativity: The Unanswered Question', while providing a general context to the book, is a commentary on the paradoxical times in which we live. In an increasingly complex business environment, the capacity to acquire and use knowledge and creativity is the only key to international competitiveness, productivity, growth and a better quality of life. This in turn requires thinking across boundaries of conventional wisdom, categories and disciplines, integrating many perspectives that achieve a balance between the inner and the outer, the local and the global. From the organizational point of view, it calls for creating a new set of skills and values and a mind-set of interdependence that can survive in multicultural, multidisciplinary situations. In short, the time is ripe for a great explosion of creativity. For these reasons business corporations are now willing to look outside traditional business disciplines for insights and guidance in fostering organizational creativity. In the last two decades a whole range of new methods and approaches has been adopted for tapping and releasing creative potential at work. Dreamwork is emerging as one of them.

This takes us to the third chapter, which in the first part

examines in detail the design, process and method of conducting a typical 'Creativity-2000' workshop. This title is a metaphor for the kind of novel approaches we may need in the next century to stimulate creativity. It discusses a step-by-step approach to dreamwork. In the second part it offers a toolkit for those interested in working on dreams individually or in teams. This will tap your own creativity as also enhance your ability to foster creativity in others. The process often reaches the depths of awareness and connects with an inner dimension that may elude us in the corporate world. When integrated with or without complementary training initiatives, such a workshop can serve as the vital link between individual and organizational transformation.

The fourth chapter, 'We Shape Our Dreams and Our Dreams Shape Us', establishes the connection between dreaming and creativity. Throughout human history, dreams have been the impetus behind many inventions. There are a number of well-documented scientific discoveries and artistic creations inspired by dreams, indicating that many dreams reflect a form of sophisticated thinking, problem assessment and problem-solving.

If dreaming is universal and creative, you may well ask how is it that the linkages between various dimensions of dreaming and the process of creativity are seldom recognized. There are several reasons for this.

First, we tend to focus more on worldly accomplishments and less on our inner capacity and consciousness. This perhaps explains why we do not fully utilize the powerful but little-used capabilities of our dreams. In this chapter I therefore venture much farther to establish the hidden link than I generally do during my workshops.

Second, dreams seem strange from the waking point of view, because during sleep the mind expresses itself in pictures. We do not draw pictures of our ideas when awake: we use words. If we are taught to understand the meaning of pictures as we are taught to understand the meaning of words, then dreams would not appear so strange.

Third, dreams typically speak in a language of symbols and metaphors. Metaphors, symbols and figures of speech are an outcome of the cognitive process that encourages new ways of thinking and perceiving. The thinking requires 'getting out of the box' of governing beliefs. Questioning and then changing governing beliefs often lead to creativity and innovation and to the possibility of fundamental rather than superficial change. Research has already indicated that many instances of creative acts are grounded in metaphors.

Similarly, there are many facets of dreaming that facilitate creative thinking. If the measure of creativity lies in the ability to make novel connections between disconnected pieces of information, ideas, insights, etc., then dreaming provides abundant scope. To begin with, a workshop helps the participants to formulate the right kind of questions. It then provides a retreat into the unconscious through the process of incubation. Incubation is an important ingredient of creativity, because it gently leads the dreamer from the logical world to the visual world, where the unexpected can be chanced upon by bringing together head and heart, in an atmosphere of mutual trust and shared enrichment.

No one knows where the borderline between creative and non-creative behaviour lies; in fact, to suggest that a sharp borderline exists is probably incorrect. But there are essential abilities for creativity:

- Sensitivity to problems and patterns of behaviour
- The ability to make connections between thoughts, memories, past experiences and associations
- The ability to respond flexibly to situations
- Recognizing the relative importance of the various elements of a situation
- Finding similarities among situations in spite of differences and drawing distinctions among situations in spite of similarities
- The ability to make sense of ambiguous and contradictory information
- The ability to generate alternative solutions

The fifth chapter, 'When Corporations Start Dreaming', discusses how the power structures within organizations are changing with increasing global interdependence, mobility and the use of information technology. Small teams within organizations are often empowered with resources in technology, manpower, materials and finance to achieve the corporate mission. They are also given the freedom to make decisions and find solutions to problems. Towards this end, new models of organizational development are being explored, models that incorporate the values of personal excellence, creativity, social responsibility and shared dreams. We therefore need to orient organizational systems to facilitate the move up the scale from cognitive knowledge (the know *what* or know *how*) to self-motivated creativity (know *why* and care *why*). From the organizational point of view there are many ways to stimulate creativity, and dreamwork is certainly one of them.

This brings up an enormous question: How do we create an organization that is responsive and receptive to the need for change? How can we fashion corporate environments where thoughts and energies harmonize and creativity is unleashed?

No doubt, change is never easy as it can leave many people within organizations hurt and bewildered because they have invested heavily into the earlier system. Further, fear of the unknown can fossilize into organizational inertia. Although the old command-and-control model of executive management is no longer sustainable and change is necessary, organizations do need to understand that the passion for change must be tempered with compassion for those affected by the process of change: they need counselling, training and healing. Are there any models that can help us deal with the fallout of change and enable us to create a climate in which collective creativity can flourish?

The fifth chapter answers these questions through a case study of Engineers India Ltd. It also explains how dream-sharing groups can create that cordial environment within a corporation wherein *collective creativity* can blossom. When corporations start dreaming, organizational systems gradually shift from 'structure orientation' to 'process orientation' and develop a greater feel for systems thinking.

The sixth chapter, 'Seeking Solutions in Sleep', presents experiential dreamwork as an alternative model for stimulating individual characteristics conducive to creativity, as seen from the experience of Indian managers in business. This experience indicates that the process of dreamwork becomes catalytic in revealing certain psychological traits in a dreamer that are associated with a creative personality. In fact, dreamwork can be instrumental in reducing the polarity between dreams, which reflect the dreamer's unconscious state, and creativity as experienced in the conscious state, by integrating them into a harmonious relationship.

The next chapter, 'The Royal Road to Empowerment', points to the fact that traditional support systems no longer offer compelling answers to the questions that women in management face today. Based on experiential material taken from workshops exclusively designed for women in industry and business, I describe how working on dreams empowers and enables women managers to take life-changing decisions. The process of dreamwork has been able to give them a new insight and skill in dealing with the stress that comes from the simultaneous demands of career and family. For many, dreamwork often succeeds in bringing about the attitudinal change so necessary for problem-solving in a shorter time than other methods of executive development.

The eighth chapter, 'Dreams of the Future and the Future of Dreams', shows how dreamwork creates a sense of bonding and community among people of diverse cultures. For the past several years I have had occasion to attend and present papers in international conferences organized around the world on the study and application of dreams. This gave me the opportunity to work on the dreams of people of diverse cultures. Based on this experience, I have come to believe that the dream experience is a refreshing way of enhancing our interdependence as members of one global family, liberating us from individual schisms, cultural constraints and geographical identities. Experiments in social dreaming such as these help bridge national boundaries, encourage mutual exchange and enrichment across cultures, and open up a whole new world of shared visions.

So, this book is for the dreamers across cultures who believe in translating their dreams into reality. Once we learn how to 'catch' our dreams, it becomes easier to bring them to reality. Moving beyond notions of cultural imperialism, dreamwork furthers our understanding of the emerging global culture of common humanness and humanity.

For managers, this book should certainly help identify specific practices, skills and disciplines that can tap their creative potential. But dreams cannot be confined to any particular discipline. Dreams cannot have any imposed boundaries. Interconnectivity is in their very nature. In this book, too, while we begin this exhilarating journey on the creativity route, we will find ourselves ending up on the consciousness route. Similarly, we start with a focus on corporate executives but will discover that the art and practice of dreamwork can be equally relevant to other professionals, as was amply demonstrated by the members of a dream study group who met once every month over a period of three years representing a variety of professions, such as those involved with education, law, medicine, detective work, and the media.

TWO

Creativity: The Unanswered Question

O N A BRIGHT sunny morning, thirty top managers from business and industry have come together for a specially designed workshop. This is hardly unusual. This kind of relaxed time away from the workplace is invaluable. It provides an opportunity to focus on problems, reflect on experiences and plan for positive action.

But there is a difference. These managers are not gathered here to discuss business process re-engineering, total quality management or financial restructuring. They have taken time off to delve into the mysterious world of dreams in order to stimulate business creativity.

While excitement is palpable in the rest of the group, Mr Mehta, president and chief executive officer of a fast-growing, multi-unit, airconditioning company, is clearly ill at ease. I recall what he told me the previous night over the phone:

'I am about to launch a joint venture in collaboration with a known partner. The project proposal is drawn up, capital investments are worked out, risks and responsibilities are well considered. The preliminary market survey is quite positive. But I continue to feel uncomfortable about this decision which, rationally speaking, appears sound from every business angle. I wonder why I do not have the usual thrill and excitement I often experience at a launch. This one currently stands postponed. Something is bothering me. But what is it? The feeling of unease and pressure is mounting every day. The project involves big money. It is a question of two million rupees. I know I cannot go on like this indefinitely. I have registered for your Creativity-2000 workshop with this specific purpose in mind, you see. Do you think we can find an answer to my question by the end of the workshop?'

Dreaming to a deadline? Has anyone ever delivered a dream on demand? 'I do not know,' I had wanted to say. It is like casting a net wide into the sea and waiting for a catch. One can only do the right things and hope for a good haul. Dreams may provide answers to problems we are ready to acknowledge or show the direction where an answer might be found, but they cannot guarantee a solution where no solution yet exists.

'Let us cast our net wide and wait in readiness to catch the right type of dream,' I had said, crossing my fingers.

The next morning we were in for a surprise. Mr Mehta was temporarily put on hold by Mr Ray, who volunteered to work first because he had woken up from a very frightening dream. His dream had jolted him awake and he had had difficulty in getting back to sleep.

The setting is the courtyard of my childhood home. There are two gunny bags on the floor. These are stuffed with something and tied with a thick string. Next to them are two children who are covered and tied with coir mats up to their necks. Their faces are uncovered.

From the corner of my eye I notice a wriggle in the gunny bags which eventually develops into a slow movement. The bags slowly start rolling from one side to the other and I realize to my horror that they are stuffed with people, half dead and gasping for breath. Gradually, the movement in the gunny bag is slowing as if life is going out.

I rush to an old, ugly shrivelled-up man who is sitting nearby and cleaning utensils nonchalantly. I demand, desperately, 'Hey! Can't you do something? These people are dying. Can you get me a knife or something so that I can cut the strings

*of the sack and set them free?' He shakes his head. 'I must
finish my chores first. Go take help from someone else.'*
I woke up with my heart palpitating with fear.

'Can you not do something?' I echoed the statement from the
dream, with emphasis and emotion.

'I have to,' he said resolutely, 'or I will die of suffocation like
the people in the sacks. It is a do-or-die situation. I resigned
from my job early this month and am serving the notice period.
Since I was nominated for this workshop much earlier the
management decided to honour the earlier decision as a sign of
goodwill, a sort of farewell gift. I have just three months to get
organized or I would be eating out of my savings. How am I
going to feed my family? This is the question that continuously
haunts me. Yet I am going about my daily routine pretending as
if everything is fine.

'I am allowing myself to be talked into a consultancy which
I find totally unexciting. I am vaguely aware that it will not do
justice to my talents and experience. At a deeper level, this is
something I do not want to happen. But outwardly I am going
along with the proposal. I must stop seeing this old "friend"
of mine who is influencing me in a big way. He is selling this
consultancy to me. I know I must limit my friendship with him,
however unpleasant that might be in the beginning. I am aware
that a deep crisis is likely to develop in my life if I do not take
charge of it.'

Clearly, this dream acted like a wake-up call that demanded
giving immediate attention to something that was going radically
wrong in Mr Ray's personal life. Fortunately, he was courageous
enough to be open about it. He realized that although the friend
was kind and well-meaning, he was pulling Ray into a sense of
negative complacency, a sense of numbness. 'It's all right. I can
manage it. Something will magically work out,' Ray was telling
himself. The dream told him what he was up against, which
encouraged him to stay strong and vigilant and immediately take
up the job offer at hand, which he had been ignoring against his
better judgement.

When this emergency was dealt with, Mr Mehta could talk about his 'prize catch'. His dream was not only vivid and rich in meaning, it had come at a pivotal decision-making point in his career.

In the dream he saw himself travelling along a rough and bumpy road leading to a narrow rickety bridge over a deep gorge covered with snow. His prospective business partner was standing at the other end, which to him appeared to be a dead end. What struck him in the dream was the implications of the dead end. This, combined with the imagery of the frozen lonely landscape and the rickety bridge over a deep hidden gorge, stirred up disturbing memories of the past. While connecting the dream to reality, he began to recall a number of half-forgotten incidents that he had failed to take into account. An alliance with the same partner many years earlier had been short-lived and turbulent due to a clash of interests and strategic intent. He realized with a jolt that he was about to repeat a counter-productive pattern. To be ignorant about an existing problem was understandable, but to continue to ignore it, once identified, was unthinkable. The issue basically was of strategic partnership, not of the investment of a huge amount of money, or even of the success of the joint venture.

However trivial it might have appeared to others, the dream spoke of his most troubling concern, the most crucial question. After all, our perception of what is important at a given point of time is always very subjective, very personal.

A fortnight later he called me up. 'The dream was like a godsend,' he said. It made him reconsider his decision. He abandoned the proposed joint venture in time with a tremendous sense of relief.

He had managed to dream on schedule after all! This is not something strange. Whenever there is a yearning in our heart or a question in our mind, an answer is usually available provided we are ready to listen with an open mind. We need to know how to tap the vast resources of knowledge contained in the inner recesses of our mind. We need to be always receptive to the responses to our questions, which may come from anywhere and from anyone. The answers may come from deep within ourselves or from the environment around us. Sometimes they may come in the form of a dream. Sometimes the answers may be in the very nature of the problem. At times, they may even challenge what we firmly believe. The transformative forces operating within us not only provide answers but also alternative solutions. Once we open the inner doors of our mind, we will find ourselves at the threshold of creativity.

In fact, seeking answers to existential concerns through the medium of questions and answers is an age-old phenomenon. The *Prashna Upanishad* (in Sanskrit *prashna* means question), for instance, derives its name from the questions asked by the seeker and discusses deep existential problems through this medium. The nature and scope of these questions may have changed from the seventh century BC the period to which the Upanishads reach back, but we have still not found complete answers to many of our critical questions—questions about who we are, where we are going and how we can deal with the emerging realities in a creative way.

When knowing is experiencing

'Without the global revolution in the sphere of consciousness, nothing will change for the better in the sphere of our being,' proclaimed Vaclav Havel, the Czechoslovakian President, addressing the people of his nation. Strange as it may sound in an era governed by technological breakthroughs, one might still argue that the human mind has not developed sufficiently to recognize and deal with the impact of these mind-boggling changes. It still functions at a relatively unsophisticated level of awareness, mindfulness and self-knowledge. This is primarily because we often believe that the basis of knowledge is experience. We usually gather knowledge from the experiences of the waking state, believing that that is the whole truth. But the Upanishads tell us that life includes the four states of consciousness—waking, dreaming, deep sleep, and the transcendental fourth state—each with its own world of experiences. They also speak of the waking state as being only a part of life and therefore the experiences gathered in that state are only partial. Hence, knowledge derived from the waking state can lead only to partial truth, not to the whole truth. Thus, knowledge of science or speculative thought—in other words, knowledge derived from the waking state alone—tends to fall short of the whole truth.

One of the foremost thinkers of his time, Roger Bacon was the pioneer of the concept of knowledge gained through experience. He stated that there is a difference between the collection of information and knowledge gained through actual experience. In his *Opus Maius* of 1268 he says: 'There are two modes of knowledge, through argument and experience. Argument brings conclusions and compels us to concede them, but it does not cause certainty nor remove doubts in order that the mind may remain at rest in truth, unless this is provided by experience' (Shah 1964). Shah further elaborates by stating that modern science, instead of accepting the idea that experience is necessary in all branches of human thought, takes the word in the sense of 'experiment', in which the experimenter remains outside his experience.

Thus scientific experimentation has confined its attention to rational, objective knowledge which is replicable, measurable and open to empirical verification. Scientific knowledge often relies on the five senses for its raw data and ignores the evidence of inner experience—the subjective experience which is non-replicable. The intuitive perceptions of reality and vast ranges of extraordinary human experience, which have the power to change our lives, emerge from deeper layers of consciousness and bring within their purview direct experiences of the physical world, without going through the intermediary five senses. For example, in the field of psychoneuroimmunology there is evidence to suggest that the body's immune system is affected by images and thoughts in the mind itself and that the power of the human mind is such that it can affect the immune and endocrine systems. Similarly, research on creativity reveals that there is a part of the mind that regularly comes up with creative solutions, artistic creations and deep wisdom not accessible to the waking mind and not learned through the physical senses (Sorokin 1962).

The knowledge that is derived from separate studies of the states of dreaming and deep sleep reveals only the partial truth, if it is not treated with a refined reasoning. When the experiences of the three states are integrated, one obtains a composite picture of reality.

The understanding of reality arrived at through the study of the three states does not conflict with or contradict any other form of reality; because the whole comprises the parts it is not in conflict with them. Without this realization we would be totally incapable of destroying the illusion that we are all separate entities.

The creativity premium

The fundamental paradox of the present is that the human race is poised at a point where influences of different cultures and climates meet, mix and integrate. Just as the advances in information technology are bringing together people from virtually every nation, culture and ethnic group, the models, metaphors and methodologies so far restricted to a specific discipline, industry or culture are becoming relevant across disciplines, enabling the emergence of a new paradigm. Ideas are shared, global alliances are forged, as the world is integrating itself at an unprecedented pace. Learning is no longer limited to a given place or culture— it is available to the entire global family. At this turning point, we are caught in the cross-fertilization among different periods, cultures and provinces of knowledge, indicating a change to a new world order. It is evident that the time is ripe for a great explosion of creativity—not by a single Einstein, Edison, Raman or Tagore, but by humanity as a whole, where every individual will need to contribute.

Koestler in his seminal work, *The Act of Creation* (1964), affirms that all individuals have the capacity for creative activity; but this is frequently superseded by the automatic routines of thought and behaviour that dominate our lives. It is when we allow rational thought to be suspended, as in dreams, that we are at our most creative.

Creativity has often been taken to be a mystery. How Newton devised a revolutionary, scientific theory and how Bach composed music in a way that has moved listeners down the ages has eluded human understanding. Creativity has always been associated with flashes of genius and with geniuses. This assumption puts it out of the reach of common people. For most, this limiting assumption also creates a gap between creative potential and actual performance.

Creativity is at a premium as never before, as the business world moves toward deregulation, private initiatives and global markets. Free-market economies, export, and value-added production are buzzwords today in former socialist or heavily protectionist countries and regions, such as China, India, Vietnam, Eastern Europe and Russia. Trade wars are replacing cold wars and free-trade areas are supplanting military zones of influence. Product cycles are becoming shorter, while computerization, telecommunications and information-processing are becoming increasingly pervasive.

The notion that technological progress and material growth will provide answers to many of our dilemmas has been completely dispelled. We are now confronted with the paradox of tremendous advances in technology on the one hand and erosion of spirituality and morality on the other. Together with the sweeping tide of globalization that is erasing the boundaries between nation and state, we also see the emergence of religious fundamentalism, fragmenting the very sense of community of nations. Epoch-making events such as the collapse of communism and the unification of Europe indicate that a new world order is emerging.

In a social research survey conducted in the US, the sociologist Ray (1996) documents how we are seeing the emergence of a new integral culture—a new constructive synthesis of modernism and its antithesis, traditionalism—a synthesis that moves beyond both while not rejecting either. It manifests a distinctive tolerance of ambiguity beyond the either/or paradigm. It is concerned with values focused on spiritual transformation and ecological sustainability and the emergence of the feminine principle.

What Arnold Toynbee (1947) found in his study of the growth and decline of the world's great civilizations is equally applicable to the world's great corporations, if we regard the corporation as a living organism passing through the inevitable stages of growth, maturity and decline. Toynbee discovered that civilizations in decline were consistently characterized by a tendency towards standardization and uniformity. In contrast, growing civilizations were characterized by a tendency towards differentiation and diversity. So it is with most corporations.

Finding meaning at work

Most of us work in organizations that have become exceedingly depersonalized; they freely lay claims to the mind and muscle and ignore the heart and soul of their employees. As a result, energy levels are low, cynicism is high and work fails to fulfil or excite. The business culture built on hierarchy and competition and developed over decades of the success of such models often divides an individual's spiritual life from his institutional life. The advance of modern industrial culture has left vast numbers of people in a state of spiritual and psychological alienation. The bewildering pace of technological change, the dominance of huge impersonal business institutions and the competitive modern society have left many feeling isolated, with no purpose or meaning to their lives. The earlier grip of religion has loosened in modern secular society. In such a scenario what is needed is a non-deified, non-religious spiritualism that enables corporate goals to resonate with the inner meanings that most people seek in their work, or, alternatively, seek in the full context of their lives. Finding meaning at work when corporate goals are fixated on quarterly earnings and shareholder value might be construed as the ultimate paradox. During periods of huge layoffs and corporate restructuring, employees feel uprooted, bewildered and cynical. They miss the sense of community, the sense of belonging. If they can find meaning in their work, that will enable them to zealously rededicate themselves to achieving corporate growth.

There is a growing realization that the roots of our ecological and interpersonal crises must lie in the attitudes, values and basic world-view we have come to hold. The boundaries that exist in the world are merely projections of our internal walls. For instance, different departments in corporate systems are not merely functional divisions; they also represent the way we think and speak. The way we conceptualize ourselves, our problems and endeavours, fundamentally influences our thinking and emotions.

The psychologist and philosopher William James observed: 'The greatest revolution in our generation is the discovery that human beings, by changing the inner attitudes of their minds, can change the outer aspects of their lives.' Never was this profound statement more true than in the present.

Most of our business life is organized around airtight logic, numbers and figures that must always be 'correct'. However, a whole range of logic-defying, seemingly irrational emotions—rage, fear, jealousy, insecurity—underlie our dilemmas, whether it is reluctance to act on a decision that appears sound from every business angle, whether it is the fear of speaking up or of speaking against a crucial matter, or the fear of failure, or a sense of ambivalence or anxiety before beginning a new project or making a huge investment. These are feelings familiar to most of us. There is a good chance that these feelings may erupt involuntarily unless we work through them. If these feelings and contradictory emotions remain unrecognized they have the power to disrupt business decisions that dreams highlight so well.

Yehezkel Dror (1968), in his study of public policy-making, writes: 'Experienced policy makers who usually explain their own decisions largely in terms of subconscious processes, such as "intuition" and "judgement", unanimously agree and even emphasize that extrarational processes play a positive and essential role in policy making. Observation of policy-making behaviour in both small and large systems, indeed all available descriptions of decisional behaviour, especially those of leaders such as Bismarck, Churchill, De Gaulle and Kennedy, seem to confirm this opinion.'

In a world where cross-cultural alliances and cross-functional teams are the norm of the day, executives can no longer afford to ignore the 'fuzzy' realm of emotions and their impact on decision-making and creativity.

A primer for developing inner technology

Strange as it may sound, in an age dominated by artificial intelligence and digital revolution, it is the universal language of dreams which is common across the globe, be it to someone living in New York or in New Delhi, Beijing or Bombay. It is a language with its own pictorial alphabet, vocabulary, grammar and logic, in which the conventional dichotomies of time and space, subject and object, self and other, are challenged in favour of integration, psychic equilibrium and the fundamental unity of humanity.

We often remember the dreams that jolt us awake, anxious and apprehensive, as in the case of Mr Ray. Often, such dreams are a reliable indicator that the dreamer's consciousness is just beginning to gain an awareness about an increasingly unbearable situation in life; a situation that demands the dreamer to fight or to flee. Such dreams can be interpreted at several levels, depending on the life circumstances and inner dilemmas of the dreamer. They can be the catalysts that spur the dreamer into action. They are new vistas to so-far unexplored ways of knowing and being.

Briefly, dreams change, integrate and symbolize elements from various areas of life. Figures of people and fragments of events come from everyday life or emerge from long-forgotten experiences. The feeling might be one we are barely aware of and therefore cannot express in our waking life. Feelings, thoughts, emotions, memories are connected in a kaleidoscope of images. The pictorial assembly of previously disconnected data about ourselves through a dream increases our chances of seeing new connections among them. The symbols in a dream often emerge from the deeper layers of our consciousness, containing seeds of information not accessible in the waking state. Each symbol is a different lens, through which much can be learned. Unravelling the meanings of these manifold images can often connect us to their life-enhancing energies. So powerful are these symbols that they could not but have emanated from some universal spirituality, as it were.

Dreams continually question and challenge norms and the assumptions we hold about ourselves, people and situations; in short, about the reality around us. Whether they challenge by provocation, as in the case of a nightmare, or evocation, as in the case of powerful imagery, dreams find ways of drawing the dreamers out of the mind-set that constrain them.

Dreams present us with a virtual world of information about ourselves, the network of our relationships, our concerns and our dilemmas. Creating value from this information requires organizing, selecting, reflecting, analyzing and synthesizing it. Just as raw material is refined into a useful product, so too can a dreamer use raw information for developing critical insights. Dreams are created in virtual space. They portray virtual reality as they act out possible scenarios, such as the simulation of potential behaviour in the inner consciousness. In many instances, as in the case of Mr Mehta, this can result in minimizing financial and emotional risks.

It is interesting to note that there are only a limited number of human issues that touch people deeply enough to dream about. These issues may revolve around attention or rejection in interpersonal relationships, obsession with power and authority, a search for identity, need for self-esteem and self-assertion, or the constant conflict between dependence and independence. In a dream-sharing group, on many occasions dreams touch the members of the group at a level of feeling which cannot be expressed in words. It will seem, then, that individual dreams with the right kind of interpretation can have meaning for everyone in the group. It is this human tendency to react in similar ways in similar situations that dreams depict so well across cultural and language boundaries, connecting people with a common bridge of understanding.

Dreaming does not require people to be of a certain colour, a certain education, a certain lifestyle, a certain class, or even to speak a certain language. Despite a multiplicity of backgrounds, dreaming creates a sense of bonding and an enhanced sense of community among people. This has been a common experience whenever I have worked on the dreams of people from different nationalities in different locations on the globe.

Dreaming is a language that has the power to speak directly to our unconscious, to the deeper layer of our consciousness, to the very source of our wisdom. Isolated, it is but a small spark; but united with others as part of a dream group these sparks grow into a flame. That strength which sustains and renews each one of us, also sustains and renews our environment. No wonder that while working on dreams in groups, one occasionally experiences a heightened sense of community, a global consciousness, with the simultaneous recognition that one is part of what one is seeing. The recognition of the personal becoming universal can give a glimmer of understanding of what Lord Krishna means when he says in the *Bhagavad Gita,* 'I am one manifested in the many.'

As we move into the final years of the twentieth century, one of the greatest challenges and opportunities facing us is to enhance our capacity to derive knowledge from multiple sources at the individual level and to explore the vast untapped sources of creative ideas at the collective level. There is a growing body of evidence that creativity can be cultivated and nurtured in individuals, groups or organizations (Amabile and Grysklewicz 1988; Barron 1971; Mackinnon 1971; Torrance 1972). We are awaiting a new cultural orientation, a new age of consciousness—one in which creativity and all forms of noetic experiences will undoubtedly play a pivotal role in business, education, healthcare and government.

THREE

Creativity-2000

W HAT KIND OF creativity will be required in 2000 and beyond? The kind that will make you stay at least two steps ahead of your competitors; the gazelle in Africa that wakes up every morning knowing that it has to run faster than every lion, while the lion gets up knowing that it has to run faster than at least one gazelle.

Creativity-2000 is a metaphor for the integration of the masculine and feminine dimensions of creativity. We know the power of the masculine principle in organizations. It is about the 'how' of things. It is about analysis, competence, expertise and mastery. It is also about form and product. The feminine principle is about the 'why'. It trusts experience. It looks at meaning and mystery. It is about the process and also about movement and growth. Creativity-2000 is a workshop whose curriculum is designed to re-balance and re-own the feminine principle—relationships, belonging, interconnectedness and interdependence—in organizations.

On the eve of each workshop, there are often queries from participants that verge on apprehension regarding the type of experience they should anticipate. 'Can this programme be compared with any other management development programme?' 'Creativity is fine, but why dreams?' This is the refrain (see Appendix 1 for frequently asked questions about dreams). Despite misgivings, the participants are eager to learn about an unfamiliar subject. This eagerness is used to advantage as a springboard to the first leap into the uncharted waters of creativity and dreamwork.

It never fails to amaze me how workshop participants, after their initial dismissal, often warm up to the process of dreamwork by the end of the second day and begin to narrate anecdotes that revolve around dream-inspired insights or events. I wonder whether this is related to the process of socialization to which children in India are subjected, which exposes them to dream-related stories. In the oral tradition, Indian children are treated to episodes from epics such as the *Ramayana* and the *Mahabharata*.

These epics incorporate many well-known dreams that establish a positive link between dreams and reality in their narratives. They have been translated into many of the languages of India and are also staged by folk theatres, leaving a deep impression on the Indian psyche. It is therefore paradoxical that Indian managers are generally capable of dismissing dreams as irrelevant and also quite willing to share something as personal as dreams. As a result, the whole group makes a dramatic shift in favour of openness and learning.

'How come Indian managers are willing to work on their dreams in a purely business setting?' is the question often asked in amazement at the end of my talks and seminars abroad by Western audiences. Dreamwork has gained acceptance in many professions in the West, but not in management and business.

The workshop design

The design of a Creativity-2000 workshop varies on the basis of the needs of the client organization. It is either offered exclusively as a two-day, three-day or five-day event or as an input in other management development programmes for up to two days. Separate designs are developed to meet varying client needs. The workshops are conducted for such diverse sectors of business as petroleum, energy, chemicals and fertilizers, engineering and computers, heavy electrical corporations and consultancy organizations.

Among the spectrum of workshop objectives, the important ones are:

- To understand the process of creativity and to explore alternative models of creative thinking
- To explore the relationship between dreams and creativity
- To detail the linkages between creativity and dreams
- To share experiences in formulating and implementing strategies for creative problem-solving through dreams
- To establish ways of fostering individual creativity in organizations

Typically, a two-day Creativity-2000 workshop comprises sessions on rekindling creativity; a dream for the corporation; dream incubation; experiential dreamwork; reading the shorthand of dreams; linkages between dreaming and the creative process; problem-solving in sleep; creating within constraints; and action plan.

Rekindling creativity

Initially, a conceptual input on creativity is given, detailing the common myths and facts based on research on the perceptual, emotional and environmental blocks to creativity and the stimulants to creativity. This is followed by a session of exercises that help to connect with the 'peak experiences' in participants' lives. They are asked to describe two events from their work experience as examples of 'high' creativity. In the first event the participants do not have to be key figures but are asked for as many details as they can remember about the event and the environment surrounding it. The second event is one where the participant played a key role. It is often observed that the critical-incident method limits statements about the personal beliefs related to creativity and brings out inspiring stories about what did influence creativity.

I have found that participants find it easier to talk about creative incidents in others' lives than about those in their own. This is largely because most of them hold the dominant belief that they do not have any creative capacities. I have met only a handful of executives who do not seem to hold this belief. In the absence of rigorous proof, even if we accept this observation, it only points to the necessity of exploding this myth.

A dream for the corporation

In this evocative session, the participants are led towards macro commitments that are larger than themselves, by asking such a question as: 'If you were to become the chief executive of the corporation, assuming there was full freedom, what will be your dream for the corporation?'

As is well known, dreaming has a personal as well as a social side. In ancient times, healers and sages across cultures dreamt for the community much in the same way as in contemporary times Gandhi, Martin Luther King and Nelson Mandela nurtured big dreams for their people. Throughout human history civilizations and communities have engaged themselves in generating dreams of ideal commonwealths when they have been in the midst of an inevitable process of decline following a period of growth.

So it is with organizations, if we treat them as living organizations. To rekindle the 'spirit' of the organization or to set the organizational 'soul' on fire, fresh dreams need to be incubated. When a dream is shared by many people it has a profound effect on the quality of their lives. It has been observed that when we dream together we can become contributing parts of a larger whole. People who share a common sense of direction and community can achieve their goals far more quickly than people who do not. This has great implications for work situations when people are working towards common objectives. In a mobile society where workplaces rule the world, and where nuclear families are often left behind for the sake of employment, it is the corporation that becomes the community for those who need a sense of belonging.

It is therefore not surprising to find that, although participants have important individual concerns and personal dreams, there is a great deal of convergence when they dream together for the corporation. For example, in the case of Engineers India Ltd (EIL) workshops, all the participants wanted EIL to be the foremost design and consultancy company. There was a confluence of imagery when they dreamt for their corporation. Such commonality of themes is seen more in the case of in-house workshops with participants from a single organization. For example, in one dream workshop for Indian Oil Corporation (IOC) conducted in February 1991, most of the dreams revolved around the theme of imminent movements and postings that generally take place in the months of March and April, and the implications of such movements for promotions and the family. Based on his experience with a particular corporation, Menezes (1992) also confirms that members of the dream group who had worked together in the corporation for an average of over twenty years seemed to have a 'collective corporate unconscious' similar to a family unconscious (Taub-Bynum 1984). It is this commonality that I emphasize in the dream workshops with the hope that it would strike a chord that would resonate into a sustained commitment.

Dream incubation

This is a time-honoured ritual of sleeping in a sacred place in anticipation of receiving a divinely inspired dream. Incubation rituals have existed in most of the older cultures, such as those of Greece, Rome, Egypt, China, Iran and India, where they are primarily used for guidance and healing. From the sixth century BC to the sixth century AD the Greeks and Romans practised 'dream incubation', which meant going to a sacred place in order to receive a useful dream from God. Most people today would not believe in the possibility of being healed in a dream. But the rationale behind the incubation ritual was actually the external-ization of the internal and the psychological processes. In other words, the dream-incubation rituals mirrored a natural inner process of self-regulation, healing and transformation.

This traditional incubation ritual has been modernized by Gayle Delaney, the San Francisco-based dream psychologist, who runs a dream consultation centre in California. I had the chance to learn the 'phrase-focusing' technique and the Dream Interview method from her in the summer of 1990. Delaney, while providing the genesis of how she developed the 'phrase-focusing' technique says: 'Many of us at least once in our lives have gone to sleep with a problem or the need for a new idea and awakened the next morning with the solution or idea clearly in mind. While sleeping on it clearly works now and then, one can develop this natural problem-solving function of one's sleeping mind by learning to incubate or target one's dreams.'

The incubation proper

The incubation session has been creatively designed by Dr F. Menezes (1987) to stimulate and integrate the active and quiet mind skills by a variety of techniques keeping Delaney's technique at its core. Together with the technique of visualization, music and meditation, this brings out the dynamic synergy of intellect and intuition. It is conducted on the eve of the first day in four stages (Figure 3.1).

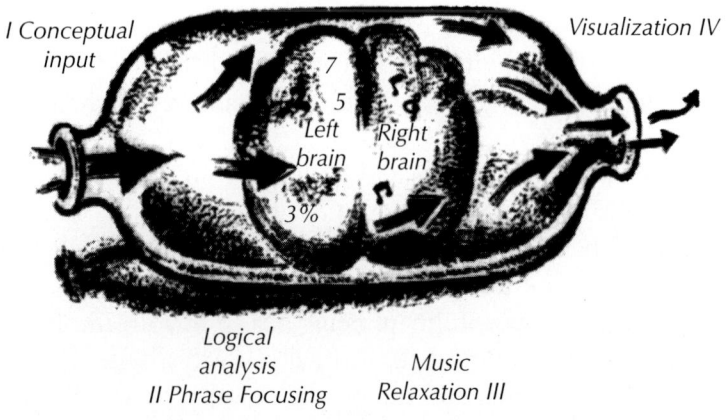

Incubation process

I Conceptual input

Visualization IV

7

5

Left brain

Right brain

3%

Logical analysis

II Phrase Focusing

Music Relaxation III

Figure 3.1 *Four stages of incubation*

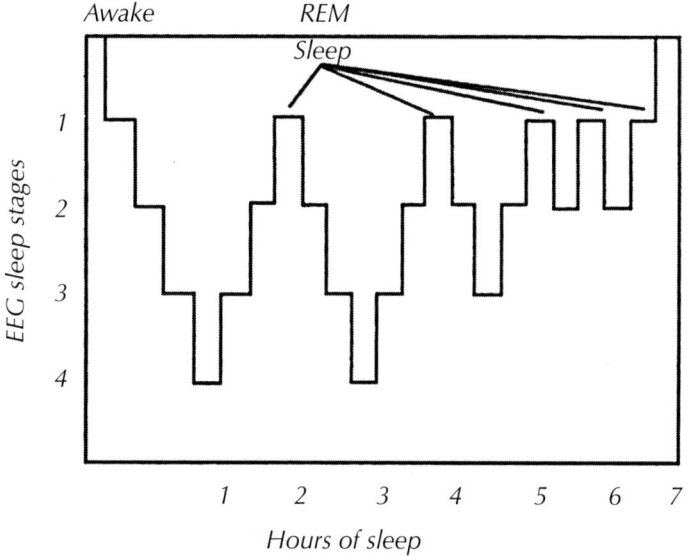

Laboratory research has indicated that dreaming sleep is found in almost all human sleep patterns in the REM stage. The REM period occurs about every 90 minutes and lasts 10 minutes just after the onset of sleep and about 45 minutes–one hour in the period just before awakening. The subject started in Stage 0 (awake) and moved successively through Stages 1 to 4 during the first hour. He then moved back through Stages 3 and 2 in the REM stage. The REM stage is like Stage 1 in terms of its EEG pattern, but it is accompanied by rapid eye movements. The width of each horizontal line indicates the duration of the corresponding stage of sleep.

Figure 3.2 *Succession of sleep stages*

In the first stage a short conceptual input on dreaming is given. It is emphasized that everyone dreams every single night and has rapid eye movement(REM)/non-rapid eye movement and successive sleep stages (Figure 3.2). Although many people do not recall their dreams in the morning, REM sleep evidence suggests that non-recallers dream as much as recallers. Dreaming is biologically important. In a normal life span of seventy years an individual spends at least 50,000 hours dreaming, that is, 2,000 days or six full years of dream time. The most generally accepted model for dream recall supports the idea that what happens on awakening is the most crucial. Unless a distraction-free waking period occurs shortly after dreaming, the memory of the dream does not register. A number of practical ways of recalling and recording have been suggested.

The second stage is the incubation proper. The participants are asked to focus on a current problem, to analyze and debate upon it, to consider its nature and origin, and to write down as much as possible about it. After much deliberation and analysis, the problem is finally reduced to a phrase or sentence and put on paper, which is placed in an envelope. The participants are asked to keep the envelope under their pillows before they go to bed. The problems are varied and wide-ranging:

'Why am I stuck in my project (career, etc.)?'

'Why is it difficult to get along with my boss (elderly subordinate)?'

'How can I get a better idea for a new marketing strategy (article, copy, etc.)?'

'How can I redesign the pipe (machine or equipment)?'

'How can I stop smoking (lose weight)?'

The art lies in framing the kind of question that is clear, precise and complete. A question that has emerged after intense examination of a problem, after considering various possible solutions and, most importantly, with a deep intent to solve it.

In the third stage, the lights are dimmed and the participants are asked to relax. A special kind of music is played which has appropriate breaks when it is suggested to the dreamers that they concentrate intensely on the phrase in the envelope to gain an insight. Music plays a significant role in relaxing the mind and helping it reach a state of receptivity.

Of late, I have also integrated the process of visualization into the incubation process, which I find very effective in enhancing dream recall. Visualization is a powerful technique, which we are familiar with from early childhood, even before we learn words. Pictorial or visual thinking is pre-verbal and very specific to dreaming and relates well with the dreaming mind which is unconcerned with logic, commonsense and convention. Koestler (1964) points out that it is visual thinking that turns out to be of great value in forging new combinations out of seemingly incompatible contexts. Most creative people literally turn out to be visionaries in that they are visual not literal thinkers. Contemporary cognitive psychologists also state that imagery has a direct relationship with the ability to invoke creativity.

Often, a strong and determined resolve to find an answer needs to be planted during the incubation session. Once the seed of *sankalpa* (a Sanskrit word for 'resolve') is planted deep into the subconscious, the collective forces of the mind bring it to fruition. This powerful seed eventually manifests into action at the conscious level.

I have observed that the answer to the incubated question may come in a long or short dream or even in a fragment of a dream. The participants, at times, report having had no dream at all. Most often, the participants awaken with a dream with an insightful diagnosis of the problem.

The incubated dream often shows the dreamer how he got into the current difficulty and how best to get out of it. This is the most important information provided by the dream. Without this knowledge we are unable to solve our problems. The fortunate ones will find the first incubated dream easy to understand upon awakening. Delaney (1981) says that this is most likely when one incubates a dream for generating new ideas or solutions to specific problems in science, project development, sports, design and habit control. In an organizational environment, the interpretation of a dream often provides an insight into a core issue and uncovers unrecognized ideas, thus facilitating problem-solving, creativity and personal development.

Learning the art of thinking in pictures

The next day the participants bring the dreams to the group. The dreams are recorded on audio cassettes. The recording serves two functions. After completing the narration of the dream the members often request the dreamer to repeat the dream so that they can pick up what they missed in the first hearing. Recording helps in preventing distortions, additions or omissions of any kind that may occur on the part of the dreamer in the second recall. In addition, this process also gives the dreamer a chance to listen to his own dream with some detachment.

The dreamer is expressing what has never been expressed before and that too in pictures. That is precisely why dreams seem so strange from the waking point of view. These are the first 'alphabets of consciousness', feelings not yet articulate enough to be translated into speech. The dreamer is transforming something vaguely felt into a visual language. He now needs help to understand the images of the dream for he is unsure about what the dream is trying to convey. For that, the dream must be shared.

Working in groups or cross-functional teams is often the done thing in an organization. The dream group (of fifteen to twenty people) provides a safe setting for dream sharing in organizations.

There are several advantages of working one-to-one in a group. First, the dreamer, who is at the centre of action, experiences an enhanced sense of community. This is because the presence of the other members of the group deepens the implications for him of what he is saying, even though the interaction may be only between him and the dream group leader.

There is also an opportunity for the person to reveal himself not only to an experienced professional but also to a group, which in a sense implies to people at large, where social acceptance or rejection is more than just a hypothetical risk. There is inherent power in the public statement of something latent or concealed, representing an expansion of one's bounded sense of self. Furthermore, this experience of the sense of community takes on the condensed power of an everyday drama, depicting not only individual but universal concerns, and heightens the sense of commonality. Witnesses to the one-to-one interaction may imbibe from it what is applicable to their own lives, and thus open up new vistas for themselves.

The group also helps the dreamer make discoveries about himself that are difficult for him to make on his own. The group is requested to understand the need for confidentiality and to maintain secrecy of the intimate disclosures and of the identity of the dreamer.

Experiential dreamwork

Experiential dreamwork, the method adopted in my work, has been developed by Dr Montague Ullman (1979, 1996), a psychiatrist extraordinaire, internationally known for his work on dreams. The process unfolds in four stages, as shown in Figure 3.3.

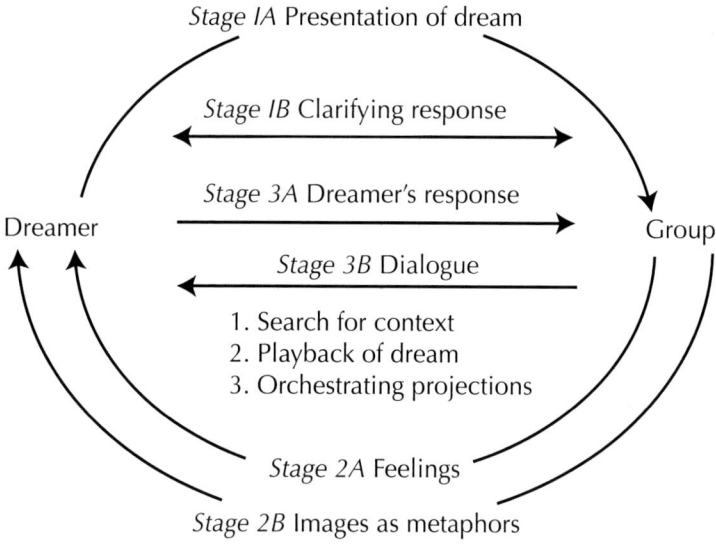

Stage IA Presentation of dream

Stage IB Clarifying response

Stage 3A Dreamer's response

Stage 3B Dialogue

1. Search for context
2. Playback of dream
3. Orchestrating projections

Dreamer

Group

Stage 2A Feelings

Stage 2B Images as metaphors

Stage 4 Presentation of any additional comments by the dreamer at the next meeting of the group

Figure 3.3 *The process of dreamwork*

Stage I A dreamer presents a dream. The decision to share a dream is left completely to the dreamer. The group may ask questions to clarify the dream and to grasp it as clearly and completely as possible. The questions are limited to the dream. Any real characters in the dream are briefly identified.

The dreamer as well as the group are asked to refrain from giving any associations or ideas about any element in the dream. At this point, the imagination of the rest of the group is not limited. This is important for the next stage where the group members make the dream their own.

Occasionally, the simple act of relating a dream to others results in a sudden insight. The very decision to share a dream implies a readiness to lower one's defences, which automatically paves the way to greater insight.

Stage II This is the stage at which the group members make the dream their own. Turn by turn, they speak of it as their own dream and offer their projections in the first person. The dreamer is asked to listen without actively participating, but he is free to accept or reject any projections of the group. The members of the group share with one another any feelings or moods that the imagery conveys. For example, 'If it were my dream . . . I feel I am isolated.' Next, the metaphorical potential of the imagery is addressed and explored. Metaphors often embody potential multiple meanings, making a wide range of interpretations possible. For example, the dreamer sees himself in prison. The windows of the prison remind him of his office windows. This can be understood as a symbolic expression of the range of feelings and thoughts the dreamer might have about the workplace; for instance, he may be conveying a sense of little or no freedom, or confinement, isolation, or punishment.

Despite the fact that at this stage the group is unaware of the events in the dreamer's life that triggered the dream, many of the projections of the members do succeed in bringing the dreamer closer to his dream. Nevertheless, questions such as 'How exactly is this place like a prison?' 'Who are the other people involved?' might lead to exploration of the deeper images related to the feeling of being wronged and/or unfairly punished.

At first glance, it might seem incredible that a group working on a stranger's dream could offer anything worthwhile to him.

But the fact is that they do. Even if the dreamer is a stranger, there are spontaneous and intuitive responses from the group members that touch him. As Ullman (1987) explains: 'There are a limited number of basic human issues (such as issues around identity, authority, power, dependence, attention) that touch people deeply enough to dream about.' Since certain similarities in people are universal, this results in an empathetic response to the metaphorical images of the dream.

Stage III The dream is returned to the dreamer who is then invited to respond to and share his understanding of the dream to the extent he is willing to.

If further work is necessary, it proceeds in the form of a dialogue between the dreamer and the group. The purpose of the dialogue is to explore the context of the dream, beginning with recent events and continuing until there is a felt sense of connection between the dream image and waking reality. Questions are put to the dreamer in an open-ended fashion to elicit more information and to focus on a specific aspect of the dream. The dreamer can deal with the questions as he wishes (he has also the right not to answer).

The first aim here is to clarify the immediate life context that shaped the dream, in the hope of creating greater clarity for the dreamer, and define the issue dreamt about. A good question to begin with is to ask if there is anything more the dreamer can say with regard to his feelings and thoughts before drifting to sleep. Also, what can the dreamer recall about the day before the night of the dream that reminds him of the events that shaped the dream. After the immediate context is clarified, the dream can be read back aloud (or played back) to the dreamer, scene by scene, to see if there is anything the dreamer might like to add. He now has a clearer perspective and understanding of the dream against the amplified context that has been elicited.

At this point another level of questioning can be introduced if the relationship between one or more images in the dream and the life context that has been shared by the dreamer with the group (the orchestration) still eludes him. If a member of the group sees a possible connection between an image and an aspect of the shared context, he can suggest it to the dreamer. Of course, the final arbiter of the fit is the dreamer, who subsequently validates or invalidates the projection.

In most stages, the control remains with the dreamer; he alone decides what to share and how much to share, with which he is comfortable.

Stage IV   At a subsequent session—which takes place in the case of a dream group but not in the case of a workshop—the dreamer has the opportunity to share any further thoughts with the group.

Experiential dreamwork in practice

The following dream, volunteered by a senior HRD manager of an engineering consultancy company, illustrates the first three stages of experiential dreamwork in practice.

Stage I   'There is snow everywhere. The landscape seems full of snow. I am rowing a canoe, a very narrow canoe, wearing a thin cap. The river is frozen too. I can see some narrow ridges and mountains in the distance. I am trying to cross a bridge with some kind of an arch, but I am stuck inbetween. I see myself as very thin and emaciated. I think of getting out of the canoe and climbing over the glacier but cannot.'

Stage II   The group worked with the dream as their own and shared the feelings and mood evoked by the imagery. The following are some of the group's responses over a 15-minute period.

'I feel helpless and frustrated.'

'I am going through difficult times, the environment is harsh and I am unable to cope up.'

'I am undertaking a difficult journey. I am alone, stuck and without resources.'

'I am in an unfamiliar situation. There is no scope for movement, mobility. I feel frightened.'

'I feel like a misfit in the situation.'

The group then worked with the metaphorical possibilities of the dream imagery. The responses of the group members given below capture only part of what evolved in 20 minutes.

'I am struggling through life. I am not settled yet. I have had enough adventure. Now I want to settle down.'

'What am I doing in this strange situation? In this harsh environment?'

'I am under stress, all alone, completely inadequate to meet challenges.'

Stage III The dreamer listened to the group's responses with rapt attention and admitted that what the members said evoked very strong feelings in him.

'I was troubled about the way I was stuck in the dream. I now realize that the dream probably depicts the way I feel about my job,' he said.

At this point the dreamer looked ready for dialogue. 'Can you say anything more about the way you feel about the job?' I asked. The dreamer confessed that he had changed five jobs during the first ten years of his career. Changing jobs rapidly had seemed like an adventure sport to him then. For sometime now, he had been suffering from insomnia on account of his inner conflict, unease and stress. His incubation question was: 'How can I get sound sleep?' Although the dream appeared seemingly unconnected with the issue, the dreamer confessed that his sleeplessness was related to unhappiness with his job. With dreamwork, he now felt as if he was in touch with something meaningful and revealing.

This often happens in dreamwork. The unconscious has its own priorities. It tells us what we really require, while the insistent clamour of 'desires and wants' wrestles with the conscious mind. Dream-driven discovery like any other discovery is full of unexpected outcomes and revelations. And, importantly, we could even chance upon an insight or discovery. Insomnia was a direct outcome of the stress he experienced at work. The undivided attention and empathy of the group members as against the dreamer's often harried and hectic life, was in itself refreshing. He felt enriched and healed to some extent by the very process of sharing his dream. Admittedly, there was still a great deal of work to be done, but the dreamwork had given him a direction which he considered very valuable at that point of time in his life.

Reading the shorthand of dreams

There have been instances when even after having worked on the dream through the group process the dreamer finds it difficult to connect with an important image of the dream that might hold the key to the mystery of the dream. In such cases, Delaney's (1981) Dream Interview method proves very useful.

The Dream Interview method of interpretation emerged from Delaney's frustration with dogmatic applications of psychotherapeutic dream theory and of her conviction that a universal activity such as dreaming should not require a psychotherapist to interpret it. Like reading or speaking a foreign language, dream skills can be taught to anyone who has the motivation and discipline to study and practise it seriously.

This method helps dreamers discover what they feel and think about their own dream imagery on the basis of structured questionnaires rather than have their dreams interpreted in an authoritative manner by a therapist. By asking the dreamer questions that explore dream images and reveal their metaphorical similarities to people and situations in his life, the Dream Interview method avoids forcing the dreamer into preconceived ill-fitting interpretations.

The dream interview can be taught as a practical skill in educational and professional settings where problem-solving and creativity are highly valued. It is amazing how quickly participants pick up dream interview skills in small groups. This method is particularly useful when one cannot seek advice from the group members after the workshop. For this reason it is one of the effective self-help methods with a 'take-home' element.

Linkages between dreaming and the creative process

The linkages between dreaming and the creative process are often not clearly perceived. In this session the elements common to dreaming and creativity are discussed. For instance, through dreaming we are able to transcend the perceptual blocks to creativity. Dreams make connections among disparate thoughts, memories, associations and ideas through unusual or fantastic combinations that reveal unexpected possibilities. Dreams speak in a language of metaphors, which play a pivotal role in the process of creativity. Most importantly, dreams are bifocal. They make simultaneous statements about the dreamer's current life situation and future possibilities. Also, the process of incubation itself—which is at the core of the workshop—is an important element of the creative process. The linkage between dreaming and the process of creativity is discussed in greater detail in Chapter 4.

Problem-solving in sleep

In this session, caselets are presented of men and women executives who have used understanding from dreams to take turning-point decisions in their lives. These executives range from those working in hard areas of business, such as R&D and operations to soft areas, such as public relations and personnel.

Creating within constraints

This exercise stimulates business realities in a macrocosm. It is conducted on the lines of a 'treasure hunt', for which the resources are all hidden. The teams have to locate the resources and compete with each other to complete the task in a given time, since environmental constraints to creativity, notably lack of freedom, adequate resources, support and recognition, is a theme frequently mentioned in organizations.

This exercise creates a setting in which the given resources have to be optimally utilized, sometimes even shared between the competing teams in a order to complete the task. In the process, there can be instances of friendly 'sabotage' of competing agendas, and mild conflicts. This can often also lead to a lot of fun and laughter.

Action plan

Most people have ideas. A few make them happen. However, it is not enough to come up with a good concept; it must be commercially viable too.

This session helps the workshop in firmly integrating ideas with the reality of the marketplace. It deals with the practical aspects of how to map out one's own plans to make that idea work, how to make it attractive to others, how to create markets within the organization, and how to be persistent and fight for it.

Toolkit for dreamworking: Catching the tail of your dreams

Here is everything you wanted to know but were hesitant to ask about catching the tail of your dreams. But before you get started, overcome apprehensions if any on the usefulness of dreams. To begin with, you need to recall and record your dreams.

Recalling your dreams

- Keep a pen and paper or a tape recorder next to your bed.
- Make a conscious resolve to remember your dreams with will-power and feeling.
- Repeat your resolve several times as you are slowly drifting off to sleep.
- Review the events of the day from the time you wake up to the moment you are about to sleep.
- Write down a few lines about what you did and felt today, with greater focus on the emotional aspect. In fact, your notes can be as short or extensive as you wish. These notes will later provide a clue to the meaning of the dream that is to follow.
- Make a deliberate effort to lie quietly, not even turn over, when you wake up in the morning. This will help you stay with the images and the feelings of the dream, because when there is movement in the body there is invariably movement in the mind.
- Upon waking, think back to the night rather than ahead to the day.
- Note your mood on waking—whether it is good or bad, happy or sad. It often offers a clue to the meaning of the dream.
- Remember, if you do not write down the dream immediately upon waking, even if the dream is vivid, you might lose some of its details or the dream altogether.

- Despite these efforts, you may not remember the dream the first time, but that should not dishearten you. Practice and persist for a week or two and you certainly will remember.
- Even if you do not remember your dreams for two or three days in a row, do not get anxious. Anxiety does not aid dream recall. If the message of the dream is significant, it will visit you again. Also, do not get so anxious about remembering dreams that you are unable to fall asleep.
- The ability to recall sometimes gets affected when you are under great work pressure or stress of any kind. It also gets affected if you have consumed medicine or alcohol the previous night. Be persistent, relaxed and patient.

Recording your dreams

- Record dreams, thoughts, feelings and impressions of the night either if you wake up during the night or in the morning.
- Record whatever you remember, even if it is just an image or a dream fragment. It can provide valuable insights. Even seemingly boring and bizarre dreams have something to convey.
- Initially, also record the date of the dream so that you can connect the dream episode with the significant event of the day. Should you decide to take a sustained interest in the dreams, this will prove useful. In the beginning, the correct interpretation of many dreams may sometimes elude you. But the insights will probably fall into place several days or even months later.
- Sometimes you may remember two or three dreams of the same night. Record and number them in their order of occurrence. Dreams of the same night generally have a common theme and revolve around the same issue.

Dreamworking with Delaney's Dream Interview method

In recent years there has been a shift of responsibility from professional to individual care with regard to promoting optimal health and well-being. Turning to our dreams for leading a more fulfilling life is a step in that direction. Delaney's Dream Interview method facilitates 'self-help' in that the dreamer actively participates in the exploration of his dreams.

When you do not have the advantage of the group but would like to continue working on dreams by yourself, the Dream Interview method developed by Gayle Delaney is a practical and concrete one for understanding the metaph orical language of dreams. I use this method for teaching practical skills during the course of my workshops. The results are rewarding on account of its simplicity and efficiency.

Delaney's method of dream interpretation uses a series of focused questions in an interview format (see Appendix 2) (something business executives can easily identify with) to elicit definitive descriptions of dream images and actions. It helps the interviewer relate with seemingly abstract dreams throughout the process.

In this interview, the interviewer (you can have a friend interview you) pretends that he has come from another planet and is curious to discover what life is like seen through the eyes of the dreamer or vice versa.

The interviewer tries to suspend any personal knowledge, belief, opinions and associations regarding the images in the dream, no matter how well he happens to know the dreamer. The dreamer is asked to define each of the settings, people, objects and events in the dream with the help of a questionnaire. As described below, diagramming the five major elements of the dream helps the dreamer concretize the dream:

- Place a box around the setting
    Setting :   e.g., house, prison
- Place a circle around people and animals
    People and animals : e.g., mother, cat
- Place an underline under the objects
    Objects: e.g., table, pen
- Place a cloud around feelings
    Feelings: e.g., angry, sad, happy
- Place an arrow under actions
    Major actions: e.g., running, talking

Take for example, the following dream.

I see myself at the foot of a snow-capped mountain. I have come here with the purpose of mountain climbing. I wonder why I am wearing bathroom slippers. I am frightened at the prospect of mountain climbing. My friend Neal is also there with me. He smiles and gives me a copy of the Sunday Times, then walks away.

This sample dream interview is based on Delaney's Dream Interview method and comprises an elaborate questionnaire. An abridged version of the interview is as follows:

Highlight feelings

Interviewer (I): *What do you feel at the end of the dream?*

Dreamer (D):   I feel frightened, nervous.

I: *Have you felt this way—frightened and nervous—recently?*

D: Not that I can think of.

Settings: Description and bridges

I: *Describe the setting of the place.*

D: It is an outdoor setting. It is a breath-taking, overwhelming kind of place.

I: *How does it feel to be in this setting?*

D: I do not like it.

I: *Does this place remind you of any place in waking life?*

D: Not exactly. But the hills behind the industrial zone where our factories are situated remind me somewhat of this setting.

People: Description and bridges

I: *Who is Neal? What sort of a person is he?*

D: He is a friend of mine. He is competent, a go-getter. He likes to rag me for my easy-going ways. For example, I like to read, listen to music, etc., in my free time. Like him, I am not into adventure sports of any kind.

I: *Does he remind you of someone or of something in yourself? If so, how?*

D: Well, he reminds me of my boss who often says that we must take on challenging projects to keep our competitive edge. He is actively considering a new project. I do not think we are fully geared for it. Our technology is old. We need a complete overhaul of technology.

Objects: Description and bridges

I: *What are slippers? What function do they serve?*

D: They are a type of footwear to wear within the house.

I: *What are the slippers in your dream like?*

D: They are blue. Much like my worn-out bathroom slippers. They badly need replacement. They are certainly not the right kind of footwear for mountain climbing.

Actions: Description and bridges

I: *Describe the major action in the dream.*

D: I am frightened at the prospect of taking the major action of the dream, which is that of climbing a mountain. I do not know how I am going to accomplish that feat in my bathroom slippers.

I: *Does this remind you of anything?*

D: Yes, this new project my boss is talking about seems like a challenging proposition. An adventure sport like mountain climbing. The fact of the matter is that we do not have adequate resources. I have not been able to express my reservations due to my need to please him. It would mean a tremendous amount of work for the next two years. In the dream Neal reminds me that spending time leisurely reading the *Sunday Times* is more characteristic of me.

I: *Now, how do you understand the dream? Is it any clearer?*

D: Yes, it does not seem strange anymore.

As can be seen from the above example, the dream revolves around feelings which form a bridge to other long-forgotten residues of the past and activate relevant memories of critical incidents.

In the process of recapitulation, the dreamer gets to hear his own words replayed to him in the context of his dream by the interviewer. This creates a distance, a perspective, in which easy recognition of one's own dynamics is possible. Insights thus generated lead to their quicker adaptation in waking life.

A simplification of the process has been presented here in order to convey the flavour and a basic understanding of dreamwork. Interpreting longer and more complex dreams, however, requires much expertise.

How to build dream teams within organizations

Dream teams can be formed by people who have a common interest in dreams, write them down at least once a week and who are ready and willing to learn from them or know more about Ullman's process of dream working (Ullman and Zimmerman 1979, Ullman 1996). What is important to remember, however, is the fact that dreamwork is serious business like any other business; at a minimum it requires investment of time and energy to yield maximum returns.

In general, the effectiveness of a dream team depends on four principles.

- That the one who has experienced something is more expert in it than the experts.
- That shared experiences and desire for change can bind us with one another.
- That mutual confidentiality and commitment are to be honoured.
- That everyone participates but no one dominates.

Each participant is a resource because he brings his talent and experience to the group. In fact, the participants together create a pool of knowledge and wisdom of which they partake and to which they contribute in equal measure. In that sense, working in a group can be extremely instructive because it offers an opportunity to learn from diverse perspectives. Also, it provides a unique opportunity for witnessing the difficulties others run into when they cannot see the obvious.

Skills

I have often been asked whether extended multidisciplinary training is required before one begins dreamwork. It would certainly help but it is not critical, albeit an aptitude for such work is much more important. During my workshops, I have come across many 'naturals' who take to dreamwork as easily as a duck takes to water. This happens because they have the basic human capacities such as sensitivity, empathy, and people orientation, and the ability to deal with ambiguity, paradoxical thinking and metaphors. With practice, discipline and commitment, these skills can be further developed.

Size

The size of the group has a bearing on the feasibility of putting the principles into practice. A group of five to eight people genuinely interested in working on dreams is ideal. Although one can begin with a group of four, a small group does not ensure against absentees. More importantly, it reduces the power of group dynamics to a great extent.

Frequency

The frequency (and time and place) of meetings can vary from team to team, but whatever time span is agreed upon, it is important to maintain regularity. After trying out weekly and monthly meetings, I have come to the conclusion that fortnightly meetings are more functional and practical. The duration of a session could be between one and two hours, which is sufficient time to follow up on the issues generated by the dreamwork of the earlier session and to work on a fresh dream at a leisurely pace.

Confidentiality

Confidentiality is imperative in a dream team. All the team members must have strong confidence that whatever is discussed during the course of dreamwork is not revealed to anyone outside the group without the prior permission of the dreamer.

Closure

Of course, even the most exciting dream teams do not stay together forever. They break up because members get transferred or develop new interests, or feel competent enough to work on their own. In such situations, it might be appropriate to call an end in consultation with all team members. However, you might acquire a friend with whom you can share and explore your dreams whenever you like.

Guidelines for team members

1. The decision to share the dream in the group rests with the dreamer. No one should be pushed or pressurized to share a dream.

2. A fresh dream (of the preceding 48 hours) is best to work with. A recent dream is preferable to an old one because it is fresh in the memory and the dreamer finds it easy to connect with actual events—unless the event was so unusual that even if it is an old one it is etched in memory.

3. Short dreams are preferable to work with within a given time constraint than long ones that sometimes take on epic dimensions.

4. The dreamer is the final authority of the dream. The right to share a dream, disclose any information related to the dream, and to call an end to the discussion at any point so that he can carry it on by himself rests with the dreamer.

5. The dreamer also has the final say on the possible meaning of his own dream.

6. It is important to remember that the dream team is not a place to go to with a hidden agenda of any kind. It is not a place to resolve interpersonal or interdepartmental conflicts. It is also not a place to iron out differences or tensions already existing between members. The basic agenda must be to learn about dreams and the universal language of dreams. The prime motivator must be nothing but mutual interest in dreams.

Dreaming to a deadline

Meeting deadlines is a harsh reality in the world of business. But deadlines are also integral to planning and execution. To be effective, they must focus on and around a critical and pressing business issue that is timebound and of a manageable size. Despite its regularity and frequency, each deadline is unique in the way it creates tension for all concerned. If we transform the tensions, doubts or fears into faith that spurs us to understand and act, we may have a dream that sheds light on a vantage point from where the course of action is crystal clear. Here, the paradox of the human will comes into play: most often, especially in moments of great tension or anxiety, the only way to be in control is by relinquishing it.

To begin with, we can relinquish control in sleep, when innumerable mysteries unfold. Sleep is a great friend, philosopher and guide, willing to work for us with no strings attached, silently, and outside of our awareness. No wonder when we wake up in the morning there is greater clarity about unresolved issues. Sometimes we also chance upon new directions. Many scientists and artists have realized the value of targeting their dreams. Einstein, for instance, used to religiously keep notepaper beside his bed to record dreams and maintained that dreams were indispensable for fundamental insights, while Kekule's 'Let's dream gentlemen' was an invitation to retreat into the unconscious. This is the kind of retreat that affords us a glimpse into the unconscious, the supreme matchmaker of the memories and associations that lie dormant in the mind. Thus, dreams stir up associations and bring them to life in strange combinations. Often, things fall into place when we wake up in the morning. This happens by chance, but we can prepare the mind in such a way that chance favours it again and again. These chance occurrences can be studied by organizing them into rather functional waking models. Dreams can serve as a 'window' on the virtual processes whereby strategies for behaviour are being set down or modified.

Incubation most often can act as a catalyst to problem-solving. Rooted in the live, ongoing, palpable concerns of the person, it puts him into situations where he must confront the blocks to progress or movement. The phase-focusing method of incubation is an excellent way to focus on an immediate concern. In the maze of priorities, it tells us what to tackle first. Further, it enhances our sensitivity to the complex issues around us.

Incubation provides a direction to problem-solving in such a way that it can at times minimize the element of trial and error inherent in the process of seeking a solution. The whole process, however, works very subtly. One must learn to look for a dream image that represents a satisfying solution to the incubated problem. But like any other method, it requires motivation, discipline and practice. Here is how:

1. Write a couple of lines about an approaching deadline or a current issue or pressing concern that is coming to a head. What do you think are the difficulties in meeting the deadline? Are there any alternative courses of action you would like to explore at this point of time? Why aren't one of them feasible? If you are in tune with your feelings regarding the issue and examine your thoughts while awake, then there is a better chance of seeing a meaningful relationship between them and your dreams.

2. Write a one-line phrase or question that clearly states what you would like to know, not asking for facts but seeking a solution, a choice or an option through a dream. For example, would it be best to release a non-productive subordinate or to transfer him? Maybe you could even draft two or three incubation questions in order to set priorities and choose a final question from among those before going to sleep. It helps to frame an open-ended question beginning with 'How', rather than 'Why', which often leads to a dead end. Since we do not have the answers to many of life's riddles and mysteries, all we can do is learn how to deal with them.

3. Repeat the incubation phrase to yourself as you are drifting off to sleep. Focus on the phrase and continue to return to it if you get distracted. The more motivated you are to meet the deadline and the more open you are to learning something new about an issue you apparently know well, the better your chances of success on the first try. The phrase-focusing method indirectly helps dream recall too.

4. When you wake up in the morning, record your thoughts, impressions, feelings of the night or the dream if you remember it. In other words, write down whatever is on your mind even if it has no apparent connection with your incubation question. Many people are unsure about which problem to incubate because they are often preoccupied with two or three competing issues and hence, unable to decide or prioritize the issues. That is why even seemingly unconnected dreams will have something to tell.

If you are lucky, the resolution to a problem can be as direct as in the case of a computer programmer of Oil India Ltd who, while working on 'Oil Comnet'—a computer network that links all the oil companies in the petroleum industry—could not remember a certain command necessary to go back to the main directory from the subdirectory, where classified data is stored. He tried out all possible commands and even checked the manual. Finally, he gave up in exasperation. Back home, this issue continued to bother him because this information was required first thing next morning. He meticulously followed the incubation procedure. In the dream that followed he saw himself sitting before the computer trying out different commands. Then, one command flashed on the screen. He woke up realizing that what he had seen in the dream was actually the right command. This was confirmed the next morning.

However, for most people dream images are metaphorical. Since it may require some work to interpret those images, it is important not to jump to conclusions about the relevance or irrelevance of the dream.

FOUR

*We Shape Our Dreams
and Our Dreams Shape Us*

WHAT HAPPENS in the mind of a scientist when he proves a hypothesis, or a writer when he is writing, composer when he is developing a theme, or a painter when he is painting? Although creativity is a product of a conscious process, it is not the product of this process alone. Clearly, a combination of factors produces creative achievements in science, literature, music, biology, medicine.

Assimilating knowledge, accumulating new facts, exploring, experimenting, developing techniques, skills, sensitivity and discrimination are all part of a conscious process. But there is a large part of the creative process that takes place in the unconscious. Like the growth of the child in the womb, it is an organic development. It dispels the notion that neither creation nor creativity is governed by wish, will or expediency.

Creation begins with a vague restlessness, a confused excitement, a yearning, a hunch, a dim cloud of an idea, an image in a dream, or an obscure intimation of an imminent potential solution. At times a new idea, insight or invention might appear spontaneously, without any apparent preliminaries, at other times it might come in the form of a mere glimpse, a fragment of a whole, or a rudiment; only in rare instances does it come in a final form, requiring only expression, elaboration and verification.

Indeed, creativity is a two-way process between the conscious and unconscious. And dreams can serve as a bridge, a meeting point for the conscious and the unconscious, the literal and the symbolic, the explicit and the tacit.

A dream is a creative phenomenon, a symbolic expression of a feeling or an experience. Dreams delve into our storehouse of experience and bring a fresh perspective to events and situations in life. Working with dreams therefore enhances our knowledge about ourselves.

The dreaming mind, which is not bound by logic or convention, creates an orientation to divergent thinking. The process of dreamwork further consolidates this orientation. It creates enabling conditions for suspending rational thought and for acquiring instead a greater fluidity and versatility of emotion and imagination.

Through descriptions of the conscious and unconscious processes that are addressed and integrated during dreamwork this chapter offers several perspectives on developing a state of mind conducive to creativity. It also draws a linkage between dreamworking and the process of creativity by focusing on each of these processes.

Are we asking the right question?

In a Peanuts cartoon, Lucy came out with her placard, 'Christ is the answer!' Charlie Brown followed with his placard, 'What was the question?'

Although it is commonly accepted that asking the right question is the first step in the process of solving a problem, it is rarely recognized as being the most important one. This is so because we generally do not define the problem or go to its root; we tend to speak of the 'problem situation', in which one or more issues are often interlinked. 'But a problem only arises when life is seen fragmentarily. If we can really understand the problem, the answer is not separate from the problem,' says the thinker and philosopher J. Krishnamurti. In other words, often, it is not lack of insight into the solution but lack of insight into the nature of the problem that impedes problem-solving. Also,

Figure 4.1   *Rind, by M.C. Escher (wood-engraving, 1955).*

the more familiar a situation, the more difficult it is to see it from a fresh perspective.

As exemplified in this book, a dream can be a pictorial statement, either literal or symbolic, of what is going on in the dreamer's life. Dream images often have a multidimensional quality and may be interpreted differently by different people. Just as Figure 4.1, a wood-engraving of a rind, could also be seen as a depiction of a human face.

Looking at a fresh dream (of the night before) is like looking through a moving, multidimensional prism. It reflects the problem from all angles, all directions, with a heightened sense of awareness. In that dynamic movement the problem suddenly undergoes redefinition. Depending on our perception and an understanding and acceptance of a given problem, the very nature and scope of the problem undergoes change.

Redefining a problem in different ways before attempting to find a solution is an accepted problem-solving strategy. It is, however, important to remember that all the right answers in the world will not help us if we ask the wrong questions. Framing the right kind of incubation question regarding our problem, therefore, is an important part of the incubation session. When we are working on a dream, we are watching an episode from our lives projected onto the mental screen and, at the same time, are part of it. This is like detaching ourselves from our own experience. A willingness to experience or perceive patterns other than those presented by the five senses allows us to take a fresh look at ourselves, to go beyond whatever restricts our vision while we are awake and reduces the perceptual block to creativity.

Dreamwork invariably succeeds in creating a sensitivity to the existing problems, nagging concerns we often do not want to acknowledge in the waking state. However, it is common in dream workshops that if the question is not properly framed, dreams sometimes reflect concerns other than those related to the incubated question. This takes the dreamer by surprise because he does not see any apparent connection between the problem to which he sought a solution during incubation and the dream the morning after.

Why does this happen? Human beings have a remarkable mechanism for self-healing that seeks equilibrium and integration. We often fail to ask the appropriate questions about what bothers us because in the waking state we concertedly deny or suppress the concerns that are stressful to us. But the unconscious has its own priorities. It throws up the problem we *must* tackle and not what we *would like* to tackle. Therefore, dreams that are not related to the incubated questions seek to harmonize what we *require* and what we *desire*. These are signals from the unconscious to be acknowledged, not problems to be ignored.

People deal with stress in different ways. This is due to personality variables. Hartman (1991) explains two ways of dealing with stress. The 'thin boundary' way of working through stress by a variety of methods and connecting it with the rest of consciousness, and the 'thick boundary' way of walling it off, keeping it out of consciousness, or denying the existence of the stress or problem altogether. This can explain why different people focus on different concerns while formulating the question in the incubation session.

For example, in the incubation session in one of the workshops, a chief public relations manager of a multinational company expressed concern about career advancement. The incubation question was also related to the same issue. However, he was surprised to report the following dream, which in his opinion was not related to the incubation issue.

The scene is a supermarket area. There is an office party going on there. Everyone is having a good time. Some are dancing and drinking too. The atmosphere is one of general merriment.

I am in a low mood. This is unusual for me, because at parties I feel quite happy and spirited. Even my colleagues find it unusual. I stay away from the crowd, with a drink in my hand. After a while, I say 'What the hell' and join in in the dancing. Suddenly, someone points to my pocket which is full of coloured pens. Apparently, it is an unusual sight because it infuriates me no end. 'How come these sets of pens are in my pocket?'

The person who noticed the pens points to the one who had quietly put them in my pocket. That person turns out to be an elderly, docile gentleman from our office, one most unlikely to do such a thing. Sitting quietly in one corner of the supermarket, apparently his job is to sort out coloured pens, which he is doing with great seriousness.

I get even more infuriated that a person like him has done this to me. I rush up to him and ask him whether he put the pens in my pocket. He looks quite guilty and admits to having done it. 'Why do we not get on with the party and forget about it?'

He carries on sorting the pens. This makes me angrier still. I throw all the pens onto the floor. This shocks everyone. The dancing and music come to a halt.

Suddenly, someone comes in and announces, more pointedly to me than anyone else, 'We should hurry because Ajay's (a colleague from the Calcutta office) wife is very ill. We should go and see her.'

'What happened?' someone asks.

'His wife has suddenly started assuming the dominant role, a role her husband used to play. A reversal of roles has taken place and that is why she is in hospital.'

At the time the dream occurred, the dreamer was working for a multinational company and was posted in its industrial township. He enjoyed his job, and was given recognition for his performance and a promise of career advancement. But then he discovered that both his parents had developed cancer. Being the only son, the onus of their care and treatment was on him. Since specialized cancer treatment was not available at the industrial township, the local hospital referred his parents to a well-known cancer hospital in Bombay. This meant that he too shift along with his parents to Bombay.

The Bombay office was small and mainly served as a liaison base. There was no scope for future advancement there. The choice was difficult. His dilemma continued to grow in intensity.

It is during this period of uncertainty that he attended the dream workshop.

The dream opens with a party scene, pointing to the fact that the dreamer enjoys his job. In the middle of the party an elderly gentleman, whose only role is that of provider, creates confusion by keeping coloured pens in the dreamer's pocket.

The dreamer had no difficulty in identifying the elderly gentleman as his father. In fact, the dreamer felt guilty for holding his father responsible for upsetting his carefully organized work scene by his illness. Apparently, a reversal of roles had taken place. The son who had been dependent on his father until then had to perforce assume the dominant role and take care of his parents, placing their interests and needs before his. Unable to cope with this conflict, the dreamer throws a tantrum in the dream, expressing pent-up rage, that he could not vent in his waking state.

The same motif is repeated in the second scene, when he receives the news of the hospitalization of his colleague's wife. In reality, Ajay's case was similar to the dreamer's. Ajay had had to seek transfer to the Calcutta office due to his family problems. There was no scope for progress there. The dreamer feared that the role reversal might handicap his career just as it had Ajay's.

The dream reflected a much larger existential concern than the dreamer chose to deal with in the incubation session. It revolved around the core issue of self-advancement versus duty and responsibility towards his parents. The group presented a novel option: to look for another job—keeping parental treatment as the first priority, which everyone in the group agreed was a harder option. It was clear that the dreamer was determined to put an end to the dilemma. Interestingly, none of the group members had any expertise to deal with such existential dilemmas, but each of them had an intelligent mind, a wealth of life experience and a warm sensitivity to the dreamer's problems, all of which served to deepen his sharing and dream experience. The dreamer decided to act on the option suggested by the group.

A follow-up eight months later indicated that the dreamer had successfully acted on this option. He initially took the transfer to Bombay, keeping parental treatment as the first priority and subsequently found another job. Clearly, when a question is held in the consciousness long enough and is viewed in a holistic way, it provides a solution that can be instrumental in changing our lives.

The retreat into the unconscious

'Man cannot persist long in a conscious state,' wrote Goethe, 'he must throw himself back into the unconscious, for his roots live there.' Highly creative men and women widely separated by time, location and specialization hold that after following a rigorous professional discipline one has to let go the reins of the conscious mind and wait for the unconscious to take over, which happens usually in a period of relaxation (Fabun 1970, Garfield 1974, Osborne 1963, Poincare 1924). If preparatory work is a necessary condition for the emergence of creative insights, then the period of incubation serves as a sufficient condition. Wallas (1926) proposed four components of the creative process: preparation, incubation, illumination, and verification. The incubation session is crucial to the workshop. It offers an opportunity to retreat into the unconscious after formulating the question related to one's problem. The play of music and light, blending of breathing and visualization, create a condition whereby a twoway traffic between the conscious and unconscious is opened up.

Creativity is sometimes characterized by flashes of illumination, which might appear in the waking state or in a dream, and is often preceded by a long period of reflection on a specific issue. For instance in science, August Kekule's formula of a benzene ring, Elias Howe's model of the sewing machine, Neil Bohr's model of an atom, Madame Curie's discovery of radium were inspired by dreams. In music, Mozart, Schumann, and Wagner had dreams that provided inspiration to their work. Faust and Dr Jekyll and Mr Hyde originated in dreams.

Although the unconscious can be a powerful ally in creativity, one can also consciously use the power of the unconscious to gain fundamental insights.

However, most managers are more inclined towards Newtonian analytical techniques. To them dreams or intuitions are at best unscientific and at worst dangerous unless they make a point or provide insights so powerfully as to challenge the basic myth about dreaming.

For example, in August 1988, when J.M.B. Barua, Chairman and Managing Director, Bongaigon Refinery and Petrochemicals Ltd, was in charge of Oil India's Rajasthan project, Oil India was drilling its first well in Rajasthan. After completion of drilling and electrologging, the well was prepared for production testing. Interpretation of the logs was done by reputed international companies. However, the logs did not show promising prospects of hydrocarbon. Completely saturated by the problem, Barua, a geoscientist by training, had the following dream:

> I am observing the well under production testing. After the preparation when the water in the well casing is being off-loaded, I notice that the surface connections are not properly made. This develops into a virtual crisis. People are running around in a state of confusion.

> In the meantime, the inflow of gas starts, someone quickly closes the well and repairs the surface flow line to the flare. After the well is tested it produces gas. The gas flare too lights up subsequently.

Incidentally, this dream occurred before the actual perforation of the well. Barua narrated the dream the following day in the weekly operations meeting. After the narration, he sceptically commented that because the dream presaged fulfilment of the wish that the well produce gas, it might produce just water in reality. However, another geologist present at the meeting said that the well might produce gas as it did in the dream. Barua later said that his own inference typically revealed his approach to decision-making: he preferred to take decisions based on analysis of hard data and not on hunches or intuitions.

Notwithstanding misgivings, the well continued to be tested. It did produce gas, but not without initial problems in lighting the gas flare (just as in the dream). The experience here, that such a zone can actually produce oil, was subsequently transferred to the upper Assam basin and oil was found in a specific zone earlier believed to be devoid of oil. Similarly, this 'pattern recognition'—which also forms the basis of any scientific discovery—can possibly also lead to oil and gas finds in other geological basins, particularly in palaeocene and cretaceous geological formations.

In the end, Barua made a powerful point that although most often dreams are forgotten, this particular dream made an impact and influenced the plan of operations because, first, it was remembered and, second, it was narrated and discussed in the meeting. Hence, clearly, dreams do not have intrinsic value. Rather, their value is derived from how we understand them, respond to them, and act or refrain from acting with regard to them.

This idea can be traced right back to ancient Indian texts of the seventh century BC on the interpretation of dreams. The basic concept that dreams reflect reality and that they bring about reality—as pointed out by O'Flaherty (1987)—is often seen in these texts. According to the *Atharvaveda* (*AV*), if one sees a series of dreams but does not remember them, these dreams will not bear fruit (*AV* 68.21.22). This suggests that it is the dreamer's awareness of the dream that brings about its results. The dream can trigger the beginning of a chain of causes or be the result of such a chain. Sometimes it is a pictorial representation of an event that is likely to happen. In such cases the dream is simply a curtain-raiser of a future event.

From logical to magical

Even in this century of Freud and Jung, working on dreams is often considered mystical or mystifying, and at times even akin to the supernatural or occult. This is more so in business and industry, where there is greater stress on logic than on understanding and dealing with emotions. In an attempt to 'box in' behaviour, managers tend to identify people with functions or departments. Therefore, anything that does not fit into 'logic', thought and reason often gets relegated to the realm of 'magic'.

There is a mistaken belief that working on dreams is not serious work and that creativity is just arts and craft largely because from childhood we are led to believe that thinking is synonymous with logic, reason and verbal expression. According to David Ogilvy, the founder director of O&M, a world-class advertising agency, 'The creative process requires more than reasons. Most original thinking is not even verbal. It requires a groping experimentation with ideas governed by intuitive hunches and inspired by the unconscious. The majority of businessmen are incapable of original thinking because they are unable to escape from the tyranny of reason. Their imaginations are blocked.'

Rich visual imagery and symbolism essentially form the magical aspect of any creative act. 'Magic' derives from the latin word *'magica'*, which connotes an inexplicable influence that produces unforeseen results or events by the occult control of nature and spirits. When an art or discipline transcends its boundaries, it goes into the realm of magic. For instance, in the language of everyday experience we speak of being moved by a performer who can weave sheer magic with his music.

Creativity is an extended process of experimentation, mistakes, mutations, and accidents. In its initial stages, there is also disorder and chaos because creativity cannot be planned, programmed or managed. But it cannot blossom without calling into question established structures of logic, reason and order. Surprise, chaos, excitement are all part of it. In a state of heightened emotion, a spark of revelation as it were, closes the gap between the conscious and the unconscious, between the known and the unknown, between the rational and the emotional, and what is experienced is almost like a magical happening. For example, Lowen Fields' studies have shown that each of us passes through a stage of 'naturalistic perception' that characterizes also the evolution of vision from primitive man to modern man. He holds that in creative activity the visual sense 'relinquishes its primacy' and universal symbols come to dominate the very process of seeing (Barron 1971).

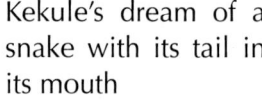

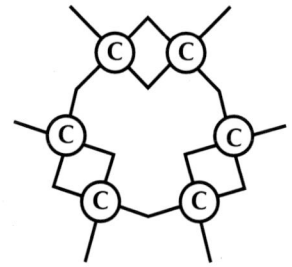

Kekule's dream of a snake with its tail in its mouth

Kekule's interpretation of the dream to mean the structure of a closed carbon ring as given in his *Textbook of Organic Chemistry* (1861)

Figure 4.2 *Kekule's dream*

The significance of pictorial thinking best emerges from the dream of Kekule, a nineteenth-century German chemist. In the course of his research into the molecular structure of benzene, he dreamed of a snake with its tail in its mouth. Kekule interpreted the dream to mean it was a closed carbon ring (Figure 4.2).

While addressing the Annual Convention of the German Chemical Society in 1890, he said: 'Perhaps it will interest you, how I arrived at some of my ideas. . . . Let us learn to dream, gentleman, perhaps we will then find the truth . . . but let us also get them examined by our waking mind.' Needless to say, Kekule no doubt was advocating the art and practice of pictorial thinking.

In fact, pictorial thinking is analogous to the rainbow whose beginning and end points are not visible; they are left open to the imagination of the viewer. However, many well-known scientists and artists have not only 'seen' the 'invisible points' but have acknowledged their role in making the visible more tangible. This is also the role of the unconscious in making many conscious discoveries. To mention contemporary examples, the creator of Peanuts, Charlie Brown and other memorable characters, cartoonist Charles Schulz, and the creator of 'You Said It', R.K. Laxman, are brilliant visual thinkers.

Sacks (1989), a British professor of neurology, speaks of his wonder at the sign language, the language of the deaf, which is built on spatial relations rather than a mere linear structure of speech:

> The existence of a visual language, sign and of the striking enhancements of perception and visual intelligence that go with its acquisition, shows us that the brain is rich in potentials we would scarcely have guessed of, shows the almost unlimited plasticity and resource of the nervous system, the human organism, when it is faced with the new must adapt. If this subject shows us the vulnerabilities, the way in which (often unwittingly) we may harm ourselves, it shows us, equally, our unknown and unexpected strengths, the infinite resources for survival and transcendence which Nature and Culture, together, have given us.

Expecting the unexpected

The notion that chance plays an important role in the process of discovery is equally applicable to dreams. Serendipity is defined as the art of discovering an unsought finding. It refers to the fairly common experience of observing an unanticipated data or information or insight which leads to the developing of a new theory or to extending an existing one.

Andel (1992), in his insightful paper on serendipity, comments that when two or more elements—ideas, associations, memories, facts, observations, relations, insights—are combined to form something new and useful, we call it a finding. According to Heracleitus (540–480 BC), 'Unless you expect the unexpected you will never find truth for it is hard to discover and hard to attain.'

How can you expect the unexpected? How can you enquire about what you do not know? This can be illustrated by the following.

Honda introduced large motorcycles in the US on the basis of market analysis that established the demand for them. The company's salesmen travelled on small Honda motorcycles. Although the public showed a surprising interest in the small motorcycles, it did not occur to the company to sell those. It was only after the success of the large models that the small motorcycles were offered for sale. This case of accidental discovery is similar to the 'successful error' of the bad and discarded glue that transformed itself into the removable self-stick 3M Post-it stickers. In fact, we will find such parallels in our own lives if we look deeply enough.

What we explore by trial and error while awake, we do continuously while dreaming. Perhaps the primary characteristic of dreaming, as opposed to the mental processes of the waking state, is making connections. Dreaming makes connections and associations far more readily than does the waking state. Memories, images, thoughts, wishes, fears and aspirations which are kept apart during the waking state come together in all sorts of interesting permutations during dreaming. This access to information is like getting on the psychic Internet. The Latin verb *cogito* for 'I think' literally means 'I shake together'. This facet of dreaming can be termed 'kaleidoscopic thinking'. This thinking enhances the ability to take an existing array of data, phenomena, assumptions and juggle them into idiosyncratic combinations, twist and shake them, look at them upside down, from all angles and directions, shifting from one form to another, thus transforming them into an entirely novel pattern of thought. This is essential for problem-solving. Einstein said that the significant problems we face cannot be solved at the same level of thinking we were at the time we created them. So, a shift in thinking will lead to stress on the possibilities and scope in a situation rather than the problem. These are not always obvious, but usually have to be identified. Here, creative thinking is required to discern what can go right rather than wrong.

In general, the role of creativity by serendipity in science, technology and management is greatly underestimated. One of the world's foremost exponents of creative thinking, J.G. Rawlinson (1981), says that 'Dreaming should be part of every manager's way of life. Perhaps, if he allowed himself to dream a little bit more . . . the options available in problem-solving would be wider and would lead to better solutions.'

Consider the dream of a general manager in charge of industrial relations of a state-owned oil company, who was once engaged in drafting a new promotion policy for the employees. The promotion policy had to cater to two sets of employees: unskilled workmen with class VIII qualification and skilled workmen with matriculation at the induction level. After much discussion, the local union suggested raising the level of unskilled workmen from class VIII to class X at the induction level. So, the draft policy was revised to include the new suggestion. When it was finally presented to the union representatives they rejected it for fear of adverse reaction from the local population. As per the recruitment norms of public sector enterprises, certain vacancies were reserved for candidates from the local community.

The solution was nowhere in sight. After two more rounds of discussions and a sleepless night the general manager had a breakthrough in a dream the following day.

In this dream he saw two railway tracks, parallel to each other but moving at different speeds: one a fast-moving track and the other a slow-moving one. This led to the idea of creating two channels of promotion for employees with different qualifications. The policy was worked out accordingly and was well received by the union representatives as well as his departmental colleagues.

In order to succeed in a world continually governed by change a manager must keep one eye open for known findings and the other for the unknown. Koestler (1964) says that when a situation is blocked, straight thinking must be superseded by 'thinking aside'—the search for a new auxiliary matrix which will unblock it, without ever before having been called upon to perform such a task. 'The essence of discovery is to hit upon such a matrix as *Roentgen's discovery of the x-rays* or *Laennec's invention of the stethoscope*' (Andel 1992) (emphasis added).

There is a two-way information highway between the conscious and the unconscious, between two currents of perception. The outer current leads to the physical: things seen, heard, tasted, and combinations of these as we experience the environment. The inner current moves through our mind silently recording the images, feelings, thoughts and desires activated by day-to-day encounters and all such subjective mindscapes that form the genesis of experience. The outer current ceases during sleep. However, the inner current continues to weave within itself the images of the new experiences that drift before us during the dreaming state. Often, when an individual is completely saturated with the problem and throws a search command within, the unconscious responds with a sudden surge of solutions. This can sometimes lead to a restructuring of the entire mindscape.

Dreams: The metaphor-making mint

A dream speaks in the language of symbols but conveys its meaning through metaphors. 'Symbolism is one of the most fundamental phenomenon. However, it is not peculiar to dreams, but is characteristic of unconscious ideation . . . and it is to be found in folklore and in popular myths, legends, linguistic idioms, proverbial wisdom and current jokes, to a more complete extent than in dreams' (Freud 1965). But dreams have an immense potential for metaphoric expression.

Since a metaphor draws similarities between disparate ideas, concepts or even physical objects through new and striking connections, it involves understanding one domain of experience in terms of another and totally different one.

Moreover, metaphoric instruction is not direct and dogmatic but indirect and intuitive. Metaphors expressed through dreams usually reveal the hidden aspects of the dreamer's life. For instance, a butterfly with wings stuck together implies limited freedom, the beautiful turquoise earrings suggest a precious relationship (Chapter six), and the medicinal tree stands for resourcefulness (Chapter seven). These examples show us how metaphors defy rigid interpretation and transcend the boundaries imposed by accepted classifications. They can serve different purposes at different times and even function in different ways at the same time. Kopp (1976) explains it beautifully: 'Instruction by metaphor does not depend primarily on mutually determined logical thinking nor on objective checking of perceptual data.

Instead knowing metaphorically implies grasping a situation intuitively in its many interplays of multiple meanings from the concrete to symbolic.'

Hughes (1989) observes: 'Metaphor provides for the inventor a bridge from the discovered or invented to the realm of the undiscovered. Edison worked out the quadruplex telegraph, perhaps the most elegant and complex of his inventions, almost entirely on the basis of an analogy with a water system including pumps, pipes, valves and water wheels.' Being grounded in metaphor, such instances of creativity resulted in the hypothesis that the creative potential of people could be enhanced if they learned to apply metaphors in situations where new and innovative viewpoints were required.

Gordon's (1961) research on synectics revealed irrefutable evidence of the metaphorical base of creativity. For example, from the time when he was a child, Einstein was plagued by a recurrent mental picture of a man trapped in a falling elevator. It was this very image which formed the metaphorical connection that led to his general theory of relativity.

The only difference between waking metaphors and dreaming metaphors is that the former are conveyed through the verbal medium, with which we are familiar, while the latter are conveyed through the visual medium, which seems strange and unfamiliar. Dreaming metaphors demand interpretation and appreciation from the point of view of the waking state.

Often, a stray metaphor suddenly induces a chain of visual imagery in the dreamer. For instance, the image of the snake eating its own tail, as seen by Kekule in a dream, provided the hidden analogy for the molecular structure of the benezene molecule. As in the case of scientific discovery, this involves making a connection, perceiving an analogy where nobody saw one before.

Samuel Taylor Coleridge observed that a willing suspension of disbelief was necessary for the creative imagination to work. Note that he did not say that belief was necessary. Such an act creates the necessary conditions for a full exploration of experience. I would point out that the same is true for dreaming as well. All kinds of constraints are regularly violated in normal dreaming. It is in this sense that the dreams have a way of creating unusual, impossible, analogies that in fact spur creative imagination. 'Imagination' as Einstein says, 'is more important than knowledge.' It is what makes humanity move forward. However, it is creative and healthy only when balanced by reality checks. A creative imagination is required in order to raise new questions, explore new possibilities, and to view old problems from a fresh perspective. Also, passion and imagination are deeply related not merely to the sensory perception but to the quality of our dreams.

Bridging the head and heart

In the third century AD, King Ts'ao sent his son Prince T'ai to the temple to study under the great master Pan Ku. Because Prince T'ai was to succeed his father as king, Pan Ku was to teach the boy how to be a good ruler. When the prince arrived at the temple, the master sent him alone to the Ming-Li forest. After one year, the prince was to return to the temple to describe the sounds of the forest.

When Prince T'ai returned, Pan Ku asked the boy to describe all that he had heard. 'Master,' replied the prince, 'I could hear the cuckoos sing, the leaves rustle, the hummingbirds hum, the crickets chirp, the grass blow, the bees buzz, and the wind whisper and holler.' When the prince had finished, the master told him to go back to the forest to listen to what more he could hear. The prince was puzzled by the request. Had he not discerned every sound already?

For days and nights on end, the young prince sat alone in the forest, listening. But he heard no sounds other than those he had already heard. Then one morning, as he sat silently beneath the trees, he began to discern faint sounds unlike those he had ever heard before. The more acutely he listened, the clearer the sounds became. A feeling of enlightenment enveloped the boy. 'These must be the sounds the master wished me to discern,' he reflected.

When Prince T'ai returned to the temple, the master asked him what more he had heard. 'Master,' responded the prince reverently, 'when I listened more closely, I could hear the unheard—the sound of flowers opening, the sound of the sun warming the earth and the sound of the grass drinking the morning dew.' The master nodded approvingly. 'To hear the unheard,' remarked Pan Ku, 'is a discipline necessary for being a good ruler. For only when a ruler has learned to listen closely to the people's hearts, hearing their uncommunicated feelings, unexpressed pains, and unspoken complaints, can he hope to inspire confidence in his people, understand when something is wrong, and meet the true needs of his citizens. States perish when leaders listen only to the spoken words and do not penetrate the souls of the people to hear their true opinions, feelings and desires.'

This parable shows the essential qualities of leadership and of actions that define an effective leader or manager: empathy, listening ability, sensitivity to people, the ability to hear what is not communicated, complaints not spoken of are very important to develop open lines of communication and teamwork within organizations. In fact, having learnt the technical skills necessary to do a job, no other ability is more important than, what Goleman (1996) calls, 'emotional intelligence'. Strangely enough, there are no model courses available for developing emotional intelligence, although the corporate sector invests huge amounts on developing the technical skills of its human resources. We almost take pride in 'knowing too much' and 'feeling' too little.

Although the word 'compete' is derived from the Latin '*com*' which means together and '*peter*', which means seek to strive together, in practice, instead of striving together, we strive for something in opposition to others. In order to synchronize our efforts in the true sense of the word, we need the competencies to discern and respond appropriately to the emotions of people so that we can influence an important meeting, mobilize, inspire and persuade others to move towards a common vision and put others at ease in a crucial negotiation on which, organizational productivity depends. Lack of awareness of such feelings could be destructive because corporate decisions cannot be made merely on the basis of rationality. They require intuitive understanding and the wisdom gained through past experience.

In this era of globalization where hierarchy within corporations is giving way to highly adaptive, professional networks, interpersonal skills are needed as never before. This opens the way to empathy towards others' perspectives. As Goleman (1996) puts it, 'Seeing things from another's perspective breaks down biased stereotypes and so breeds tolerance and acceptance of difference so necessary in the workplace.'

In the workplace, the dream-sharing group truly represents a macrocosm of any working organization. Ullman's experiential dreamwork (as described in Chapter 3) is particularly useful from the organizational point of view. Its unique step-by-step structuring of the group process develops an active relationship with dreams in a safe environment. It also presents a rare chance for executives to connect with the much-ignored realm of feelings and emotions. In that sense dreamwork, among other things, imparts training in developing empathy and sensitivity to feelings at the workplace.

During the first phase of experiential dreamwork a dream is presented to the group. The members of the group work with the dream as their own by projecting whatever feelings the imagery evokes. Many people respond spontaneously to the feelings, while some might say that they have no feelings about the dream (which is fine, because it is not obligatory to respond).

However, some experience genuine confusion in identifying and classifying feelings. For instance: Is guilt a brother of shame? Is envy a child of anger and fear? Is boredom a product of thinking or feeling? Do we think first or feel first? In that case, there is a range of emotions to choose from: anger, love, sadness, fear, shame, surprise, excitement, disgust, guilt, etc.

These and similar questions open up a whole world of feelings which, at first glance, might have little to do with the work issue initially incubated. But expression of intense emotions eventually leads to inquiry regarding the issues. Often, the work issues revolve around broad themes of competence, ambition, identity, power, authority, ignorance, recognition and balancing work and family. Most people tend to separate them from personal issues. But when personal issues are viewed in a broader perspective, a pattern of behaviour seems to emerge that encompasses both. It becomes clear then that personal issues are deeply connected with work issues and both form a part of the same core issue— discovering and risking being more like oneself. This realization to some extent bridges the gap between emotional life and corporate life.

Ullman's experiential approach has not only taken dreamwork outside the realm of therapy and the consulting room, but has also succeeded in creating a context in which the personal reality of the dream becomes a shared reality of the group. This invariably becomes a source of learning for others.

The dream group provides what Newell and Simon (1972) call the 'problem space': not the physical environment but the conceptual space in which participants can experiment with alternative approaches to problem-solving and even risk multiple solutions. Quite often, an individual's abilities, perceptions or misconceptions limit the 'solution space', that is, the entire range of possible solutions to a problem. It is therefore important to keep the 'problem space' as large as possible because one cannot be optimally creative in a state of isolation. The creative ideas, images, the world of others can inspire people to ignite their own creative spark. Further, they enhance self-reflection and provide a direction to those who are 'soul-searching' at a given point of time. Dreams are important from this point of view, for they commemorate the seasons of the soul or a special event or phase in the soul's journey.

While we dream we transcend the limits of our personal identity. We experience the sense of being oneself and somebody else at the same time. It is like stepping out of one's skin and getting into another's and feeling what the other is feeling. This projective faculty, which is grounded in sympathy, is skilfully used in experiential dreamwork.

The greatest emotive potential of dreamwork is the universal symbols and deep resonance that certain images evoke. These images give form to formless longings and deeply felt needs and desires and lead to a virtual 'earthing' of emotions by relating a particular experience to a universal theme. What is common across these emotions is the sense of participation or identifica- tion with others. At a deeper level of awareness, the boundary of the individual state is transcended: the self is experienced as a part of a larger whole.

From the temporal to the eternal

Although Freud and Jung discovered the importance of dreams to the human psyche, questions regarding the nature and functions of dreams continued to remain unanswered until Asrensky and Kleitman's discovery in 1953 of REM (rapid eye movements) and the associated brainwaves and biological indicators that accompany dreaming. This discovery proved that dreaming is common to all sleeping organisms and occurs in respective cycles during the night (see Figure 3.1), irrespective of recall. It also answered such questions as how often we dream, how long a dream lasts, and how we are all similar in the ability to dream but differ in our ability to recall dreams.

The brain remains active day and night. At night it works like a computer during off-line processing—merging old data with the new, discarding dated information, but giving feedback by switching channels from the verbal to the visual mode. With computers came attempts to duplicate the functions of the brain by computer algorithm, which led to the brain being viewed as a powerful neurocomputer. In an essay on 'self-organization', Bremmerman (1995) observes that the brain has many 'agencies' which roughly correspond to subroutines of a program of a sequential computer. Neuro-computation during sleep is likely to attend to tasks that are incompatible with the instant attention and response capabilities of the state of wakeful alertness, when one is actively interacting with the environment, dangers and opportunities, friends and enemies.

During sleep, the mind reconciles recent events with past experiences to form a consistent body of empirical knowledge. During REM sleep, contemplated actions and their consequences are explored. Dreams indeed project scenarios of action or create new ones in response to the previous day's experiences. They enable us to test behaviour options in a safe environment from among which, upon waking and due reflection, we can choose from. Dreams often defy the laws of physics—they might feature wild animals or long-dead people; they might regress us into childhood or fast-forward us into the future. Although dreams are not remembered if a person is awakened during REM sleep, he usually reports to have been dreaming. It is the highly emotional, disturbing or puzzling dreams that are usually remembered and brought to dream workshops. Also, dilemmas which form the basis of crucial decision-making might first appear in a dream, either in a clear or hazy form. For example, how to reconcile the conflicting demands of family, tradition and career, whether to continue in a job or to seek a change, whether or not to move to another place of posting, which partner to choose in a relationship or marriage or which location to drill for finding crude oil. Even the combined forces of dream simulation and the rational mind that routinely evaluates dreams might not be able to formulate the decisions to such vexed issues. Sometimes, this is on account of difficulty in understanding particular dream symbols. In such a case, interaction with a group or an analyst or a skilled dream interpreter can be of great help.

In business, dreams can help minimize risks. For instance, if a dreamer is wondering whether to diversify into a new line of business, a dream makes a 'current' statement about his problem as well as indicates future possibilities—the consequences of his decision should he choose to act upon it. Through hypothetical simulation, dreams also explore potentially dangerous or ill-advised actions.

Computer science has found that simulation is often the only method to explore the consequences of behaviour strategies. This is as true of the dreaming mind as it is of mathematical games that rely on playing the game over and over again with different parameters. Dreams reflect a hazy form of something before it becomes active or concrete in waking life, that is, before it emerges on the conscious plane. As Jung states, 'dreams are ahead of us' and therefore they create and play out possible scenarios of important or emerging decisions. It is no wonder that dreams may sometimes even reflect bodily changes before there is a conscious awareness of them. This has been frequently noted (Breger et al. 1971, Garfield 1991 and Woodman 1993).

Woodman (1993), in fact, states that dreams function diagnostically. In several cases, the dreamers learnt about their ailments much before they were detected medically. The body is a multilingual organism; it speaks not only through the fine senses, but also through dreams. Clearly, if we keep track of our dreams, they will serve as early indicators of those issues which have the potential to develop into stressful ones.

Towards this end, the studies by Cartright (1991) on the relation of dream incorporation to stressful events suggest that those who report long dreams with anxious themes are 'psychologically immunizing' themselves in their dreams. Cartright found that focusing on dreams can allay depression and teach coping strategies. Garfield (1974) suggests that successful problem-solving in dream life carries over into waking life. Dreams can therefore be crucial learning experiences.

The ability to deal with paradoxical models is the hallmark of dreaming. It may increasingly prove to be the 'chosen' strategy for business survival in the future, which has so far been governed by the either/or strategy. 'Because the future,' as Mandi and Sethi (1996) suggest, 'will require wider, more inclusive lens, which will hold two extremes. For example, the future will be shaped not only by transnational companies but also by local entrepreneurs.' Hence, organizations will do well to simultaneously focus on short-term and long-term business strategies and to play on the 'speciality' as well as 'commodity' sides of business. And if the key characteristic is the ability to change quickly, they must remove the blinkers that reduce their view of competition to an either/or proposition.

Bower and Christensen (1995) in their award-winning article suggest that to remain at the top of their industries companies must create two simultaneous alternatives: keep their mainstream business alive and exploit the potential of new technologies and emerging markets. That calls for an exquisite balance between the ground reality of business and its potential prospects, to assure the company's future growth and vitality.

Since the ability to entertain simultaneous streams of thought is an intrinsic characteristic of dreams, it may play an important role in developing a mind-set ideal for business in the future.

FIVE

When Corporations Start Dreaming

'IT TAKES ALL the running you can do to stay in the same place. If you want to get somewhere else, you must run at least twice as fast as that,' the Queen told Alice in *Through the Looking Glass.* This could well qualify to become the corporate mission of many organizations across the world.

With the international business environment becoming increasingly competitive and changing rapidly, to get 'somewhere else' now involves a never-ending search for technological and managerial improvements and the capacity to anticipate and manage change, while 'running in the same place' is tantamount to moving backwards. Hence, corporations are setting policies for innovative action in order to respond successfully to the daily changes in business. And for this, creativity is the paramount prerequisite.

But are we really asking for innovation hard enough?

Although it is widely acknowledged that competitive advantage is gained through innovation, organizations have paid surprisingly little attention to nurturing it. In a knowledge-driven business society, the capacity to acquire, access and use knowledge from experts is absolutely essential to commercialize an innovative product or a service.

Then there is intuitive knowledge of what will work and what will not—the know-how of design engineer or an insight of an R&D scientist—that never gets fully articulated. Because such tacit knowledge is encoded with specific individuals, it never gets translated into action unless there is a crisis within the corporation or movement, superannuation or turnover of such people. Despite its enormous potential for creating a competitive edge, corporations seem to be more interested in generating profits and creating market share than in creating a knowledge base specific to their industry.

One wonders whether it is possible to achieve the seemingly disparate objectives of creating market share and a knowledge base simultaneously. Clearly, unless we find ways and means to integrate our focus, we may fast approach the point of diminishing returns. While massive enterprise downsizing and acquisitions grab the headlines, we often fail to take note of the silent incremental changes in the daily routines of business, which are too small to make headlines. Past glory, success and financial stability act as corporate blinkers that prevent managements from noticing the first signs of change; for instance, IBM's initial success and subsequent failure and later efforts to regenerate itself, and Microsoft losing its edge to the Internet. In today's continually changing environments, there can be no happy endings.

Evidence tells us that this is mainly because of corporate arrogance: 'we have done this right innumerable times' is precisely the wrong attitude for doing things differently for the first time. Behind the incredible excitement of transforming a bold new idea into a new product, there are equally incredible and grim realities of failure, disappointment and huge costs the first few times. But our business environments neither allow for intelligent failure nor do they create a climate for intelligent risktaking. Organizations are preoccupied with their struggles to minimize failure rather than learning to manage failure intelligently. Rewarding intelligent effort and giving freedom to experiment, therefore, may well lead to breakthroughs some of which are basically premised on failure or tolerance of failure.

Thus, innovative corporations create an environment conducive to creativity where interesting mistakes, intelligent failures and meaningful risks are permitted, thus paving the way for accidental inventions. Such an environment also promotes that aspect of creativity which is seldom taken into account, that is, the cumulative innovative efforts of people across departments, using each other's ideas as building blocks.

For instance, Post-it stickers, one of the top five office products worldwide, started as a bookmark during a dull Sunday sermon. Art Fry, corporate scientist of 3M, who used to sing with the choir, used bits of paper to flag off what they were supposed to sing. The paper would invariably come off, leaving Fry looking for the right page. He often thought about a bookmark that would stick where it was meant to. This set him working on devising an adhesive that would do the impossible—not get stickier, get dry or pull off the fibres of the paper.

It was after several hits and misses during the 15 per cent of time 3M permitted its scientists to work on their 'pet projects', that Art Fry, together with Silver, another scientist from 3M, devised the 'temporarily permanent' adhesive on removable self-stick Post-it notes.

Keeping the corporate 'DNA' alive

Despite the fact that learning from intelligent failures suggests a never-ending agenda, organizations isolate learning and training from each other. Most organizations spend the greater part of their training time, money and energy on developing basic and advanced skills (know-what and know-how) rather than creative skills (know-why, or the capabilities to answer such questions as: Why do we do what we do? How can we do things differently in order to gain competitive advantage or facilitate enterprise renewal?). In a business economy fuelled by intellectual rather than hard assets, the primary source of sustainable success is the company's skill, knowledge and information base. For example, in a technology-oriented business the source of competitive advantage will be its technology-based intellectual assets. Collectively, these intangible assets—including patents, trademarks, trade secrets and know-how, engineering drawings and company software—can be worth several times the book value of tangible assets. Often, the technology-based asset pool remains untapped as a source of value creation.

Training is meant to deliver high quality input for high quality performance in specific functional areas. But the paradox of corporate life is such that specialists more often than not get slotted in specialized areas. For instance, a finance expert may maintain a very narrow view of the business and have problems adjusting to different business situations. This is a stumbling block for executives in the way of developing a strategic view of the business by looking for ideas outside their specific field of specialization. The paradox here is such that developing a core competence could well lead to developing a core rigidity over time. It is innovative activities within organizations that can serve to guard against this by opening the doors to new sources of knowledge, new channels of information and new methods of problem-solving.

Although it may be true that only the most foolish of mice would hide in a cat's ear, it is equally true that only the wisest of cats would ever think of looking there. This is well illustrated by the story of Mulla Nasrudin from the folklore of the Middle East.

Time and again Nasrudin went from Persia to Greece on donkey-back. Each time he carried two panniers of straw but returned without them. Each time the guards searched him for contraband but never found any. 'What are you carrying, Nasrudin?' they would ask. 'I am a smuggler,' he would say.

Years later, and more prosperous, Nasrudin moved to Egypt. One of the customs men met him there.

'Tell me, Mulla, now that you are out of the jurisdiction of Greece and Persia, and living in luxury, what was it that you were smuggling that we could never catch you?'

'Donkeys,' stated Nasrudin.

The experts had missed the obvious!

As the business environment grows increasingly complex, the price of 'missing the obvious' could be enormous. What is required is a holistic appreciation of the multidisciplinary activities that govern any business and determine its very existence. Often, the biggest barrier in the way of doing 'the obvious' is the so-called 'proven professional expertise' that creates boundaries around professional discipline. Over time, these functional boundaries become fortified and obstruct new ideas and crucial information about emerging technology and changing markets, turning corporations into inward-looking rigid bureaucracies.

When an enterprise undergoes transformation it follows fundamental change. As Lancourt (1996) puts it: 'When a caterpillar is transformed into a butterfly, its DNA may remain the same but it undergoes a dramatic alteration. A butterfly is not a caterpillar with wings strapped to its back, flying is not simply another form of crawling, it is an entirely different form of behaviour, one that cannot be performed by a caterpillar. Transformation in organizational terms is about making multiple discontinuous behavioural changes to a whole organism.'

It is important to recognize that we are not likely to learn all we need to know about creative transformation by focusing only on success; we must learn to appreciate the various elements that led up to and enabled or increased the odds of success. These elements are usually not visible in the moment of success; also, we are unlikely to look for them or their absence in processes that are successful or in the aftermath of failure.

It is only through knowledge of the creative process and the factors influencing it that we learn how to facilitate creativity. And the creative process is equally influenced by individual and organizational factors. (The individual factors are discussed in Chapter 6.) The most notable and common constraints to innovation in large organizations are discussed in the next section.

Fostering innovation

In India, the National Petroleum Management Programme is a learning network of oil industry organizations committed to improving the key capabilities of its member organizations with the objective of helping the oil industry become globally competitive. This became necessary after the Government of India initiated a major process of reform and liberalization in 1991. One of the major consequences of the reform programme is the progressive loosening of the regulatory framework, consistent with the imperatives of global competition. The government-owned oil industry organizations, engaged from exploration and production to refining and marketing of oil and natural gas, are responding to the emerging challenges through a range of proactive strategies.

In recognition of the key role of innovation in gaining competitive advantage, a comprehensive study was undertaken in 1996 to explore past innovations in oil industry organizations and develop a broad framework of enabling factors at the individual and organizational levels for institutionalizing innovation. In order to develop a clear perspective for the proposed study, a one-day brainstorming workshop was held. Participants included directors on board from the Oil and Natural Gas Commission (ONGC), Indian Oil Corporation (IOL), Gas Authority of India Ltd (GAIL) and Engineers India Ltd (EIL), members of officers' associations, multidisciplinary experts from within and outside the industry, and apex-level policy-makers from the Ministry of Petroleum and Natural Gas.

In this workshop, some of the most critical enablers for fostering innovation that emerged were: organizational support and commitment to chosen projects, long-term strategies, interactive communication and constructive feedback; reward and appropriate incentive systems for successful as well as intelligent failures; and participative decision-making and flexible structures that encourage interdependence and autonomy.

Barriers to innovation

If these factors enable innovation within organizations, then what are those that block it?

Excessive bureaucratic structures Excessive bureaucratic structures require multilevel approvals and these cause delays at every stage. This is compounded by the fact that senior executives in big companies have little contact with the shop-floor, customers or other stakeholders who might influence technological innovation. Hence, the interactive feedback that fosters innovation is virtually non-existent. As a result, early signals of change go unnoticed, increasing real costs and risks for the organization.

Short-term focus on problem-solving State-owned companies are governed by the continuous requirement to report quarterly performance and profits. This short-term focus conflicts with the long-term focus major innovations normally require. In fact, it is in the very nature of innovations to often disrupt well-laid plans, accepted power centres, and firmly entrenched organizational practices, thus incurring high costs. Short-term focus also compels companies to favour quick fixes, cost-cutting and rigid practices over processes that would yield product or quality innovations in the long run.

Technological rigidities Organizations more often perceive themselves as by-products of technological systems. Technology, then, colours their view of business reality. Further, this view does not prepare organizations for technological discontinuities, which occur frequently and unpredictably. Hence, when the market demands a new technology, these constrained mental models create massive resistance to change, despite the availability of capital and the talent pool.

Also, technological innovation must first capture the imagination of the experts before it can capture market share because technology rests with them. Also, imaginative ideas and new technologies come from cutting across disciplinary boundaries. They are often spurred by special performance needs in one sector and later transferred to another. For example, consumer electronics display technologies are used in automobiles.

Poor nurturing of creative ideas Ideas need a great deal of nurturing and support. They are intellectual assets that need to be collected, generated, enriched, evaluated and finally prioritized for funding, programming and implementation. They need 'sponsors' within the organization; for instance, an R&D scientist from GAIL noted in the brainstorming workshop that freedom to conduct focused research within the broad framework of the corporate mission (GAIL has recently redefined its mission from being a gas transmission company to an energy company) has resulted in the filing of several Indian patents.

Interestingly, curbing automotive emission to check vehicular pollution is certainly not one of GAIL's missions. But the research team worked with full freedom on several projects and succeeded in achieving breakthroughs in developing:

- A microprocessor-based fuel injection system that would reduce emission of hydrocarbon and carbon monoxide in two-stroke engines and resultant vehicular pollution in the metropolitan cities in India
- A smoke scrubber for diesel vehicles
- A low-emission restorative fuel
- An alternative fuel for petrol vehicles

This was an unanticipated outcome—perhaps this is what is meant by creativity by serendipity. In this case, sustained funding reflected the commitment of the organization towards long-term research. Thus, organizations would do well to introduce and reinforce 'nursery' mechanisms for nurturing new ideas, and design seed programmes to ensure their steady flow. There are companies—among them Gillette, Philips, Toshiba, Hewlett-Packard—that have well-documented processes for achieving this and to provide training on how to perform to a high standard of excellence.

Over-specialization A rigid, hierarchical, specialist orientation can succeed, but only to a point. It may be good for corporate survival but not for its continued renewal.

The innovation-inspired environment of the present requires going beyond traditional boundaries to challenge conventional wisdom, which, in turn, will encourage cross-pollination of ideas, across disciplines and specialities. Similarly, collaboration across divisions within a given organization can generate new ideas and learning.

It is a paradox that those who create learning environments within organizations are the ones who have been able to transcend the boundaries of their specialized learning or training.

Non-inclusion of innovation as a core value A preliminary 'creativity audit' of the participant organizations was conducted through the brainstorming workshop, which was later reinforced by a detailed study called 'Appreciative Enquiry' by Eicher Consultancy Services. This study examined real-world, 'on-line' creativity, through detailed content analysis of interviews with a large number of people actually involved in different locations of IOC and ONGC. One pertinent question came up repeatedly: is innovation as much a core value as the value to maximize return on investment?

When an organization does not stress on innovation as a core value, its rate of planned innovation is bound to decline. There are also instances where innovation is hailed on paper but not encouraged in practice because managements are averse to taking risks and/or intolerant of failure.

Indeed, innovation is not the privileged agenda of R&D. This was made abundantly clear by the 'Appreciative Enquiry' as well. What might initially appear to be a major innovation in one aspect of the organization—namely, technology—might well have major implications for virtually all its other aspects. For example, the successful application of information technology at the corporate level is not possible without innovations in the field and other unit offices. It must therefore be kept in mind that the technical, production, distribution, human resource, financial and commercial activities are interrelated. It is ensuring their conceptual and perceptual (practical) 'fit' that is a highly complex and challenging task, albeit crucial to the formulation of wider corporate business and operational strategies.

Organizational commitment to innovation, or, for that matter, any other new business strategy, is neither achieved in a hurry nor achieved once and for all. There is doubt, frustration, despair, depression and seemingly conflicting interests. Hence, sustainable commitment to innovation calls for confrontation with the forces of denial, discouragement and disillusionment, namely, those who want to maintain the status quo, the predictable and safe way of doing 'the done things around here.'

This brings to mind a statement of Machiavelli that holds good even in the twenty-first century: 'There is nothing more difficult in hand or uncertain in its success than to take the lead in the introduction of a new order to things, because the innovator has for enemies all those who have done well under the old conditions and lukewarm defenders in those who may do well under the new.'

For instance, an oil company may want the profits that would come with the discovery of a new oil field, but is it really prepared to make the organizational and technological changes that this entails? While allocating adequate finances for exploration efforts, will it create a dynamic system that will invest into and nurture innovation and treat it as a predictable, manageable business system like any other? Will it create a culture that will institutionalize creativity and innovation?

The answers to these questions will come only later. But, clearly, it is time now for all organizations to invest into the intellectual capabilities of managers, contrary to the past practice of investing only in the physical assets to maximize returns. The job of the future manager will be to manage the intellectual assets and organize around professional intellect. In other words, we must unshackle the human brain and unleash its creative potential. For this, we will require a somewhat different philosophy and perspective of management. We will need organizations that are dynamic, with internal processes that are adaptive, flexible and creative, rather than restrictive and confining. They will still need structure and order, but of a kind that enables people to use their intellect and contribute innovative ideas in an incremental way. This is an exciting possibility.

Are there any practical ways of transforming this possibility into reality? Just as there are many paths that lead to the full development of creative potential and professional intellect, so are there many ways of making organizational environments more stimulating and productive for people. One such way is through the doorway of dreams, the key to which lies in a preparedness and willingness to shift from a structure orientation to a process orientation that demands a holistic approach to business.

The paradigm in process

From my experience of conducting Creativity and Dream workshops in diverse sectors of business, such as petroleum, energy, chemicals and fertilizers, engineering, manufacturing and computers, with participants ranging from presidents and board-level executives to young managers and engineers, I have seen that working on dreams initiates a process orientation in thinking. The process itself emphasizes and reinforces the fact that at a deeper level all human beings are connected, irrespective of apparent differences. This aspect of dreaming is corroborated by the concepts of unbroken wholeness and implicate order of beings postulated by the theoretical physicist David Bohm.

'There is an implicate order underlying the explicate order,' states David Bohm. The explicate order is often understood as the separateness as manifested in particles and entities. As a result, we think in terms of all kinds of dualities, for instance, mind and matter, structure and process. However, this separateness vanishes in the underlying implicate order in which we find 'undivided wholeness in flowing movement' (Bohm 1980).

In practice, dualism, or the explicate order that dominates ordinary experience, leads to fragmentation and separateness. It often narrows our vision and thus reduces the richness of human experience, limits options, or results in confrontation because differences are perceived as threatening. The reason we tend to believe in the structure-process dualism is that structures—a department, for example, in an organization—appear to be relatively static. The fast processes such as plant operations and communications systems in these relatively static structures further reinforce the distinction between the structure and the process. However, on closer observation it turns out that the structure changes, too, albeit at a very slow pace. The contrast between the slow and fast processes gives the illusion of a relatively static structure within which dynamic processes occur. In addition, as Sattler (1995) points out, there seems to be a linguistic reason for this distinction which is rooted in the common noun–verb structure of most languages. In this structure, the noun refers to a relatively static unit such as a structure and the verb to a process. Sattler further elaborates that the structure–process duality appears to be built into the structure of most languages and we therefore tend to perceive the world in terms of a structure–process dualism. The realization that the dynamics of a particular structure—such as departments—is fully integrated with the processes of the whole organization and the environment at large can have profound implications in promoting connectedness, cooperation and collaboration.

Translating this realization into organizational practice is easier said than achieved. It is not uncommon for departmental teams to work as if they are entities independent of the larger organizations. Also, traditionally speaking, hierarchies generally presuppose variations in the degrees of competence and abilities. To be in a position to give advice, money, expertise is decidedly empowering, while those lower in the hierarchy become frustrated by their lack of power to make decisions. As a consequence, important issues might hang fire in the corridors of functional politics.

In the course of dream workshops, participants representing the macrocosm of organizations engage in joint exploration, a mutuality in which there is no distinction between a group member and the leader, the giver and the receiver. The more meaningful the participation, the more enrichment it provides. As the participants work on their dreams they learn to see in the dreams what is not possible to see in the waking state. In the process, mistakes are made, risks are taken and lessons are learnt. There is a sense of adventure and a great deal of experimentation. While working on dreams we cannot even pretend to know where we are going. Because we are going into the mysterious unknown, going where the dream leads, a collaborative process through which possibilities are revealed rather than imposed.

I believe that our dreams can be a potential pathway to the

source of the implicate order, the interconnectedness between people. As Ullman (1979) observes: 'Group dream work discloses an agency that works against fragmentation.' It establishes trust, communion and a sense of solidarity. The boundaries of time and space that keep us apart in our waking life merge into a continuum while dreaming. So, depending on our concept of and faith in dreaming, we are able to catch fleeting glimpses of the mysteries that attunement with the implicate order can bring. Thus, sharing dreams in a group provides an occasion for reflecting on the essence of our own life and work.

Traditional creativity techniques, such as divergent and convergent thinking, brainstorming and lateral thinking, have been used earlier (Evans & Dechan 1990), but there is now a search for newer models that will reflect back to us the unlimited possibilities that lie untapped within us. This explains the willingness of many organizations to look outside traditional business disciplines for models that can enhance the creativity of their managers.

For example, Menezes (1987) writes about his consulting assignment with a large public sector corporation in the petrochemicals industry. The development efforts of this organization focused on the critical areas of performance. One such area was the Research and Development Centre. Finding the traditional methods of development inadequate, he decided to experiment with dreamwork as an instrument of change as well as a means of unblocking the creative potential of the scientists.

Dreamwork brought to the surface several issues related to the work environment, which helped identify problems at the Centre. As a result it was recommended that:

- The R&D Centre should basically consist of two groups: one engaged mainly in 'blue-sky' research and the other in specific mission-oriented research projects.
- Information on corporate plans and mission-oriented projects be freely shared with all R&D scientists.
- A few interpersonal effectiveness programmes be organized to create and reinforce a climate of trust and two-way communication.

As a follow-up, the scientists started the Dream Club. The trust and bonding generated through dreamwork has greatly enhanced the working environment of the organization.

Engineers India's experience

Engineers India Ltd (EIL), the only consultancy organization in the petroleum sector, has emerged as South Asia's leading design engineering and consultancy company with a turnover of 65 million dollars and profits of US$ 30 million and a highly qualified manpower of 4,000 people. It has carried out consultancy assignments in several countries, including the USA, Europe, Middle East and South Asia. On the whole, EIL has always functioned in a protected market. However, with the entry of many international consulting firms in India, it now has to compete with the best.

EIL is acutely aware of the challenges ahead and has gone through a process of in-depth introspection through various exercises across the company. In order to keep up with competitive pressures it is looking out for new insights to foster organizational creativity.

A series of meetings with board-level executives of EIL revealed a common concern: to become globally competitive. Therefore, I wanted to find out what kind of skills or attributes are required to become globally competitive. For an organization that has functioned in a protected market, this shift itself—in the opinion of many of the senior executives of the company—reflects substantial change in the basic assumptions of business. For example:

- From where we do business to how we do business.
- From service orientation to customer orientation and market sensitivity.
- From a specialist view to a multidisciplinary cross-functional view of business.

- From centralized management to a flexible organizational structure with greater focus on innovation.

What emerged as a common denominator in the cluster of skills is the premium on creative problem-solving ability or a mind-set for creativity imperative to organizational change. It was clear that changing these basic assumptions and belief systems would involve changing the entire system; and since people are most crucial to any system, the place to begin is with them.

For creativity to flourish in an organization, people must believe that creative potential exists in all and that it can be fostered through a variety of techniques. In fact, the most fundamental characteristic of an innovative environment is sensitivity to change. This requires organizational support and commitment to create a climate for creativity within the organization and realign the values of the organization in such a way that innovation is stated as a core value.

This was the contextual input that went into designing and conducting several workshops (see Chapter 6) as an enabling mechanism fostering a creativity-friendly environment.

Participants' profile

Although creativity orientation is required for all disciplines and departments, there are crucial questions concerning sequencing and interventions among departments. For instance, which disciplines should be integrated so as to lead to cross-fertilization of ideas in related areas? Based on interviews, there seems to be a general consensus emerging that these workshops should initially be conducted for cross-functional groups of senior managers (namely, Process, Construction, Instrumentation, Electrical/Structural, Metallurgy Engineering, Heat and Mass Transfer, Pipeline, Project Services, Quality Assurance, R&D). It is widely believed that these departments require managers with a high level of creative problem-solving abilities.

The average age of the participants was 42 years. All participants had degrees in engineering. They had been working for the same organization for 12–20 years.

A dream sample

The dreams were spurred by feelings of anxiety and concerns that the participants ascribed mostly to work-related issues, such as the need for designing an efficient system for quicker engineering estimates, restructuring norms and procedures within the system, the lack of freedom to take decisions and, most importantly, lack of freedom to do creative work that required moving out of the 'system'.

One of the socially conscious participants was much perturbed about the increasing traffic on the roads of Delhi that was causing frustrating delays in commuting. During the incubation session, he incubated a dream about a solution to this problem. His question was: 'What kind of a system will guarantee a fast and steady flow of rush-hour traffic on the major roads in Delhi?'

In his dream, he sees himself digging a tunnel, which is large enough for an underground metro. He feels that an underground metro is the answer to the maddening traffic of Delhi. But he wonders whether this gigantic task can be implemented without the aid of supernatural powers.

Escaping the stagnation of routine and of life trapped between rush-hour traffic jams, his dreaming mind flew with a sense of inspiration and exhilaration. He woke up with a sense of wonder and adventure. No matter how fantastic the solution of the underground metro sounded to his rational, waking mind, it was not as senseless or impossible. It had a bearing on his waking life, as a dream often has. He wondered what would happen, what all was possible, if he took more risks with his 'fantastic' ideas and their implementation.

The dream has a resonance at another level of his waking concern. He often experienced frustration due to the constraints of bureaucratic procedures and norms of the public sector enterprise he worked for. As a result, a job order often took anywhere between 10–12 months to materialize. In his opinion this drastically slowed down the response time as compared to that of the competitors in the private sector. Hence, he felt that massive change and restructuring of public sector norms was the only solution. The task, he felt, was as enormous as constructing an underground metro.

Even if there is an element of absurdity in the form of a seemingly fantastic solution to a complex problem in this dream, it is so because absurdity, like humour, provides a direct connection to the unconventional, the impossible, by transcending logic, reason and conventional thought. This in itself is the beginning of the exciting journey to enhancing creativity.

Lessons learnt from the workshops

A short self-report questionnaire given to all the participants at the end of the workshops yielded, among others, five interesting results. First, 84 per cent of the respondents said that they would continue working with dreams after the workshops. Second, 63 per cent said that they would sign up for future workshops. Third, 78 per cent said that they would recommend it to others. Fourth, 55 per cent felt that it is possible to enhance creativity through dreams. Fifth, 72 per cent were of the opinion that this workshop has definite application as a new method for executive education.

From these workshops emerged a number of practical suggestions from participants. For example:

- In an information-driven business world, accessing the right kind of information at the right time and the right place provides a competitive edge. Hence, greater application of information technology for establishing communication linkages between far-flung units/project offices and the corporate office and between office and home will reduce the response time to clients and develop better customer interface.
- Create smaller, autonomous units to execute turnkey projects.
- Seek modification of the public sector norms and procedures that slow down the speed of response. For instance, where possible, the responsibility for implementing the project must rest with the project-approving authority to prevent time and cost overrun.

- A more pronounced shift from specialist business orientation to multidisciplinary, cross-functional orientation.
- Create conditions within the organization that empower individuals to experiment, create, develop, test and innovate.
- Regular review meetings of project managers to share experiences, both good and bad, and learn from one another's successes and failures.
- Introduce the concept of profit sharing for enhancing individual as well as organizational productivity.

Considering that all the participants were hard-core engineers with years of conditioning and socialization in the 'masculine' paradigm, the individual learning shared at the end of the workshop is noteworthy:

- Realization that, contrary to conventional corporate wisdom, 'soft' (divergent) thinking is as important as 'hard' (convergent) thinking.
- Soft thinking, which is associated with the right side of the brain, is metaphorical and approximate, humorous, and capable of dealing with contradictions.
- The process of divergent thinking requires the same degree of hard work as convergent thinking.
- Hunches or intuition, often viewed and dismissed as 'subjective', can actually provide solutions to practical problems. Chance favours the prepared mind, but it does so only in a mind prepared by interest, thought, observation and experience.
- People are at their most creative when they are free to work at what they love. Therefore, 15 per cent of executive time should be allocated for work on 'pet projects' that could well become stepping stones for innovations. Decidedly, this kind of intrinsic motivation can influence what a person *can* do and what he *will* do.
- Dream workshops can contribute to creating environments for creativity within the organization, with dream-sharing

groups with all members participating in problem-solving, irrespective of hierarchy.
- Each employee has a role to play in mobilizing and managing innovation unlike earlier when bosses did the thinking and employees put it into practice. The core of successful management lies in the art of mobilizing and integrating the intellectual brainpower of all employees.

Although it is too early yet to draw conclusions, what is implicit in these suggestions is the need for their careful analysis by all stakeholders of the organization. However, their implementation is not at all simple. Finally, it can be said that the experience of Engineers India suggests that dream workshops successfully explode the myth that creativity belongs to the chosen new and re-establishes the fact that dreaming is as much a universal phenomenon as is dream-inspired creativity.

SIX

Seeking Solutions in Sleep

'IF ALL THE dreams which men had dreamed during a particular period were written down, they would give an accurate notion of the spirit which prevailed at the time.' George Hegel expresses well not only the essence of dreaming but the spirit in which it is appreciated.

What kind of spirit is likely to prevail in a future which is being shaped by constant change, revolution in information technology and extremely turbulent environment of globalization? Dealing with such a scenario would call for an ideal blend of the ability to seek equilibrium on the one hand and explore new possibilities of experience on the other—where the inner and outer, the intellect and intuition, the conscious and unconscious spheres of knowledge meet, mix and integrate.

However, due to the bias in our scientific and social systems against examining knowledge that is not quantifiable, dreams and intuition have so far been considered unscientific. This is primarily so because dreams have long been associated with mystery, premonitions and prophecy. It was earlier believed that dreams were messages from gods, ancestors, devils or even other planets and that they foretold the future. Throughout literature there are references to prophetic dreams and their appreciation for the purpose of moulding religious, social and political behaviour. In recent times, however, dreams have been used as a source of inspiration in all aspects of culture, art, philosophy, architecture, law, religion, science and business. For instance, there is record of a dream of Lieutenant Colonel H.R.P. Dickson, a British political agent and the real ruler of Kuwait, in 1937:

> One day, a violent sandstorm carved a hole by a palm tree in his compound, and that night he dreamed that he approached the hole and found a sarcophagus. Upon touching the shroud within, a beautiful maiden rose to life. Then he heard the shouts of some strangers in the desert who seized the sobbing girl and tried to bury her alive. Colonel Dickson chased the men away and then woke up.

Perplexed by his vision, he consulted a Bedouin woman renowned for her power of prophecy, she told him that the girl in the sarcophagus was the harbinger of riches beneath the sand of Kuwait and that the men were strangers from across the sea who wished to prevent its discovery. She said that the colonel should go to the diggers at Bahrah and tell them to abandon that place and proceed instead to the desert of Burgan. There, by a lonely palm tree, they would find a great treasure.

For two years a British team had been drilling dry wells at Bahrah on Kuwait Bay, but they laughed at Colonel Dickson when he told them of his dream and urged them to try Burgan, about thirty miles south. Undaunted, he sailed to London and recounted his dream to the company executives. One of them, a believer in dreams and prophecies, cabled Kuwait and transferred the team to Burgan. There, in May 1938, by a lonely palm tree, they struck oil.

Colonel Dickson's dream is an important document in the history of the international oil industry because it demonstrates that attaching credibility to a supposedly incredible occurrence like a dream can enrich the quality of life of an entire civilization.

This explains the soft stereotype about dreaming. Dreaming is regarded as soft, subjective, transient and private in comparison to waking life, which is hard, objective, permanent and public (O'Flaherty 1987). However, I would here like to again draw attention to all those dream-inspired discoveries of the past and the dream-driven problem-solving of today that have enriched the quality of our life. One can therefore argue that dreaming too is hard, relentlessly hard, and that it too can stand at the core of our concepts of creativity and innovation.

The dream dimensions

Dreams function in a variety of ways. The majority of them have no value other than that of recording the functioning of the brain, which remains active during sleep and responds to external stimuli. These dreams are almost always determined by purely physical circumstances: the way one sleeps, the position in the bed, the state of general health, digestion, breathing, etc.

The other category of dreams comprises those that are rooted in the impressions of the day and triggered by a chance encounter, a conversation with someone, or stray memories or ideas. These dreams may be important in their consequences because they are not governed by the constraints we impose on the way we think or feel in the waking state. They reflect the way we perceive some of those tendencies, impulses, desires or attitudes in ourselves which we may not be consciously aware of or are unwilling to acknowledge. No wonder it is said that we discover our real nature in sleep.

In India, dream classification started as early as at the time of the *Atharvaveda* (sixth century AD), which organized dreams according to the physical temperament of the dreamer, the time of night the dream took place, etc.

The medical text attributed to Charaka (O'Flaherty 1987) divides dreams into categories that cover waking experience, somatic impulses, imagination and supernatural influences. These dreams mirror what has been seen, heard and experienced in waking life, they foretell the future, reflect the disturbance of a particular bodily humour, dramatize individual fantasies or are mere wish-fulfilment.

Although there are many different conditions that might lead to dreaming, Tibetan wisdom groups these into two main categories.

The more common type of dreams are related to an event that touched the person deeply and left its traces in the form of a strong emotion. Such traces lead to recurring dreams with corresponding themes in similar situations.

Then there are dreams of clarity. These arise when the body, speech and mind of the dreamer are relaxed. Some of these dreams can even anticipate a future event. Here, the premise is that all human beings have in their real nature infinite potential and unmanifested qualities. For instance, we cannot see the sun when it is up and shining if it is hidden behind heavy clouds, but at other times we can catch a fleeting glimpse of it through the clouds. Similarly the self, which is often clouded by anxieties, fears or doubts, spontaneously emerges in a dream of clarity.

However, the most elaborate classification of dreams appears in a Tibetan Mahayana text called 'The Meeting of the Father and the Son'. In this text, the threefold classification according to humours is replaced by the threefold classification according to the three poisons: lust, hatred and delusion. The triad forms just one axis of the system, while the other consists of the five sense organs plus the sixth sense, namely, imagination.

The Buddhist work *Mrtyu-Vanchana* ('Cheating Death') classifies dreams by the three poisons and the six senses. It is argued that the psychological poison appears first in a dream and subsequently in body actions, speech and mind (Wayman 1984).

There are records of writings on dreams and of their theory and practice that date back 4,000 years. Although it is true that a dream is a personal document and is always focused on the dreamer's personal life, hopes and fears, there are dream themes that are common among people. These universal themes often crop up in workshops, lectures or even in casual conversation.

Such dreams are of falling, flying, taking an examination, missing a train or an aeroplane, of persecution (being chased), birth and death. The themes listed below are illustrative, not exhaustive, and appear in the important stages in life. They offer the dreamer a chance to deal with past or current predicaments and may present an opportunity to progress emotionally, provided one dares to look into them and decipher their meaning.

Dreams of falling

It may be a good idea to explore whether or not the dream contains some kind of message regarding a literal fall due to something we have ignored or failed to attend to over the last few days. For example, after I dreamed of falling on the pavement of a busy street, on waking I examined my high-heeled shoes and found that one heel was loose and quite wobbly. I had clearly noticed this earlier but neglected to do anything about it.

If dreams of falling have no literal meaning then you need to explore their metaphorical meaning. Have you fallen short of someone's expectations? Have you fallen in your own eyes? A friend of mine dreamed of falling off the balcony she was planning to construct but feared that she would not be able to afford. This was a reflection of her feeling that she could not keep up with her ambitions of leading a high life.

Dreams of falling—of toppling from some imaginary or real summit of achievement—might also reflect the fear of failure. Those who feel compelled to climb higher in their business or profession might experience an underlying anxiety that some 'fall' will hurl them back into the original state of fear.

Dreams of flying

The metaphorical meaning of a flying dream can take on many hues and colours. It may mirror the dreamer's efforts to rise above confining circumstances or his feeling of elation. For instance, I flew for days in my dreams after I got a first class first in my postgraduate degree course in psychology.

Psychologists often relate flying dreams to sexual desire but this would be grossly limiting their metaphorical implications. Sometimes these dreams could be related to an unusual ability the dreamer did not know he possessed, or indicate a possibility of breaking out of a restrictive space into one without boundaries.

Examination dreams

The majority of examination dreams are those in which you see the question paper and realize to your horror that you cannot answer a single question, or that you have studied for math and the paper is on history, or simply that the time is up and you still have to answer the second section of the paper. Such dreams occur when we are feeling 'tested' by some specific situation or person in our waking life.

Will I make the grade? Am I being tested on some issue in my life? are some of the metaphorical questions that reflect our feelings. Since these kind of situations are fairly common in modern competitive society, such dreams are reported in all phases of life and among people of wide-ranging age groups and positions.

Once a middle-aged, competent and promising engineer reported an examination dream in the workshop. In the dream he saw himself taking a viva voce. He was being interviewed by a tough panel and felt anxious that he would not make the grade. An MS in engineering from MIT, he wondered what the dream was all about, considering that he had no plans of taking any academic course. However, when we worked on the dream, it emerged that he was one of the candidates for board-level positions, for which there was tough competition. His anxiety was that he would be thoroughly tested and would possibly not make the grade. This example shows that it is important to relate dreams to specific situations in life for that will enable the dreamer to gain an insight into the unconscious workings of his mind and perhaps lead him towards some constructive solution.

Dreams of persecution

Dreams of persecution or being chased are frequently reported. The persecutor could be anyone from a demon, monster, thief or burglar to a wild elephant or a tiger, sometimes even just a presence in the dream.

The question is: Are you feeling endangered by someone or a certain situation? Are you feeling powerless in front of an aggressive person? Are you being driven against the wall for something you have done or for something you have not been able to do? The dream narrated in the section 'Are you asking the right kind of question?' in Chapter 4 fits into this category.

Dreams of nudity

Contrary to what is widely believed, dreams of being naked in public have nothing to do with sexuality but often have something to do with feeling exposed, embarrassed or ashamed. The expression 'lose face' signifies our fear of what will happen if others catch a glimpse of our real selves. There may be a desire or longing to be absolutely open and honest but the dreamer is apprehensive about showing his true self to the world for fear that that will result in criticism, ridicule or disapproval. These dreams often challenge the dreamer to shed the mask, the outer persona. They often bring us face to face with our inner realities or selves as a result of which we feel exposed or defenceless.

Missing a train or plane

'I ran along an endless platform, forever bumping into people and luggage trolleys but the train started to move. I ran harder but could not catch it. I saw the train disappearing from sight and felt terribly anxious.' Here is a dream familiar to many of us.

Since travelling is part of a busy corporate executive's life, the anxiety relating to catching a train or plane is experienced frequently. However, metaphorically speaking, the question is: Do you allow yourself sufficient time to prepare for a journey or an event or opportunity, or do you often feel that there is not enough time to prepare and that you are missing out on life in general? Particularly, there might be a sense of missing a chance to be on an important committee or delegation or missing a promotion or an opportunity of foreign travel. There might also be a sense of being in a state of transition, of not having 'arrived'.

Since a journey, be it a train, boat or plane journey, represents movement through life, dreams of this category are an expression of the fear that we are not progressing as we wish. These dreams may point to a current problem or the need to change our attitude in order to complete the journey and achieve the desired progress.

Dreams of birth

Dreams of birth signify anything mental, emotional, physical, that is new in our lives—a new interest, belief, relationship, assignment, project or posting, or new experience—being conceived, laboured or delivered. Our dreaming mind is asking the question: What is new in my life? Is it in my inner or external life? How can I attend to it? The age of the 'baby' in the dream (for instance, five or six months to a year old) could broadly indicate the time when a given 'new phenomenon' was conceived.

Dreams of death

Dreams of death have several different contexts, but they mostly relate to our own death or to that of someone very close to us. However, they do not signify anything ominous unless we are aware that someone is ill.

If one dreams of one's own death it usually implies a desire for revival and a fresh start. Death is also a metaphor that signifies an end: the end of a relationship or a chapter in one's life. It may indicate feelings of loss, grief, guilt or even anxiety over losing something precious or someone we care deeply for; or a parting with someone from whom we will be temporarily or permanently separated. Sometimes such dreams reveal that a significant person is 'moving away' from us in real life. The people in death dreams—including strangers—might represent those aspects of the self we either wish or fear to lose or that our feelings for something or someone are dead; they could also point to the end of a long-held value, belief or attitude. Here the question is: What is it that is coming to an end in my life, and how can I let it go? In that sense, it signifies a journey of release, renunciation and atonement. The death dream may be trying to force the dreamer to come to terms with the fact that something is irrevocably over and one must continue to go on living in spite of it.

Despite references to numerous dreams of significance in a variety of cultures, it is interesting to note that all dreams do not provide 'breakthrough' solutions or 'million-dollar' insights.

Like our thoughts and ideas in the waking state that are good at times and not so good at others, dreams too can range from the mundane to the miraculous, from the routine to the revelatory. In fact, dreams connect the two invisible ends of the 'rainbow' of creativity through 'the royal road of the unconscious'. To be able to do so at will and not just once in a while, is a challenging idea. The inner technology of the unconscious is available to all who care to learn it, and with sufficient motivation and practice, anyone can master it. However, what is distinctive about people with a high level of creativity is a correspondingly high level of integration of their conscious thinking with their unconscious.

The models of creativity

Kuhn (1988) has pointed out that research on creativity has been carried out extensively in the natural sciences, to a lesser extent in the arts and humanities, and minimally in other professional domains such as management and law. It is reported that there are striking similarities among creative processes. A creative person, besides having certain specific traits, also has especially ready access to and easy receptivity towards the inner resource—what Newmann (1959) called the creative unconscious (Mattoon 1984).

Based on his study of the personality characteristic associated with scientific and artistic creativity, Barron (1971) proposed that mature, adult creativity is determined not by IQ but by perceptual and attitudinal styles of using the mind. Highly creative individuals have a perceptually open and flexible attitude, possess an intuitive awareness of the deeper meaning of life and tend towards complexity in whatever they do. They also report a high frequency of dreaming.

This brings me to the questions frequently asked in dream workshops. The numerous instances of dream-inspired creativity make participants uncertain about their own creative abilities. Some express concern over the fact that they never dream. However, it is not that they never dream, they often do not remember their dreams. One frequent question is: 'Are not we supposed to have a break at night? We will be working overtime if we start paying attention to our dreams.'

This statement is a misnomer because we will dream, irrespective of whether or not we pay attention to our dreams. Experiments of the sleep researchers Asrensky and Klietman (1953) way back in 1952 showed that dreaming was common across all living organisms because it is biologically important. Also, it provides psychic immunization to the stresses and strains of the waking state. Hence, by paying attention to our dreams we cultivate an awareness of a silent track that can infuse joy and purpose into our lives. The experiences of some corporate executives described later in this chapter serve to illustrate the foregoing point.

Dream-driven discoveries

From among the dreams collected in the course of dream workshops and dream study groups, six categories of dreams are isolated as examples of how dreamwork helps the dreamer become aware of his hidden potential. While attempting problem solving through dreams, the dreamer is stimulated to use his latent creative characteristics. These correspond to the Snowflake Model of Creativity developed by David Perkins, co-director of Project Zero at Harvard University.

The Snowflake Model of Creativity

Project Zero has been studying cognitive skills among scientists and artists for the past four decades. Biographical evidence and abundant laboratory data on the creative personality have revealed a number of traits that are common to most creative people. Based on the study, David Perkins developed the Snowflake Model of Creativity, which corresponds to the six sides of the snowflake, each with its own complex structure. Perkins (1981) has stated that all creative individuals have six related but distinct psychological traits: commitment to personal aesthetics, sense of purpose, mental mobility, ability to work at the edge of one's competence, objectivity, and motivation. They may not possess all six, but the more traits they have, the more creative they tend to be (Gee 1985, McAleer 1989).

It is interesting to note that the resources of the mind—whether learned or inborn abilities—have to be mined and used in order to get honed. Creativity, however, is a function of our abilities. Although a creative person will notice more, connect more, analyze more deeply, exercise better judgement, and so on, these potentials are inherent in all people.

1. Commitment to personal aesthetics As a part of their personal aesthetic, creative individuals have a high tolerance for ambiguity, disorganization, and asymmetry and an appreciation of complexity. They often thrive on the challenge of cutting through chaos and struggling towards resolution and synthesis. Barron's (1971) findings, too, suggest that creative individuals prefer complexity to simplicity and order to disorder. When the dreamer brings a dream to the group, he often describes it as 'bizarre', 'mysterious', or 'meaningless'. He carries with him the uncertainty and ambiguity regarding the significance of his dream until the dream group progresses, step by step, and the meaning of the dream gradually revealed. Once the dream is explored and understood in this way, a sense of acceptance slowly emerges. Learning to live with ambiguity in a business world that expects certainty, and to probe and explore in a corporate culture that expects rapid decisions requires a unique combination of patience and daring.

Take, for example, the dream of a finance manager of an oil company:

> *Against a greenish-blue and orangish-red background, a butterfly is flying. The butterfly is golden in colour with black, rounded spots and stripes, golden tips, and black antennae. It is not a big butterfly, but an ordinary sized one. It is flying in a peculiar way—neither flapping its wings nor spreading its feet. It is flying with its feet stuck together. Then I see a cardboard box just like a shoe-box. On the back side of the box, I see an arch that reminds me of the entrance arch of our own house, which is under construction.*

While working on the dream it became clear that, to the dreamer, the colourful, flying butterfly with its wings stuck together was a metaphor for himself. In the dream he was asking himself: 'Do I stagnate in my present job or do I continue to exercise my freedom of moving from one job to another as I did earlier? Do I continue in the same way or do I settle for material security?'

In reality, the dreamer had changed jobs in rapid succession and his present job was his ninth. In the past, whenever the dreamer had become restless and felt that he was stagnating, he had experienced no restraint in changing jobs. His outlook changed when he got married (three years prior to the dream) and took a substantial loan from the company on easy repayment terms for building a house. That meant a long-term service obligation. His uneasy feelings and growing sense of discomfort that the dream revealed made him aware that he was no longer free to change jobs at will. In fact, he had unknowingly traded his freedom for an investment in long-term security. His wings were indeed 'stuck' until he repaid the loan.

The dream revolved around the core issue of freedom versus confinement and highlighted the dreamer's predicament. The dreamwork helped him cut through a maze of ambiguous images and the delusion of freedom and set his priorities in order. The learning process was painful and full of struggle. But the struggle, as the dreamer acknowledged, had led to growth, resolution and synthesis.

2. Sense of purpose Creative people invariably spend an inordinate amount of time thinking about a problem and exploring all the options for solving it before they settle for a solution. The dream of a general manager in a private retail business offers an example. At the time the dream occurred he was actively considering collaborating with his sister-in-law to start a new line of business. Even after having done all the groundwork, the dreamer kept on postponing implementation of his decision. He could not understand why he felt so uncomfortable about a decision that appeared sound from almost every business angle.

The dreamer registered for the workshop with a specific purpose in mind. He focused on the problem during the incubation session. Here is his dream:

I am travelling in a bus going out of town. I am holding my little two-year-old daughter in my arms. My sister-in-law and her husband are in the same bus, occupying the front seats. I wonder why I am standing when there are not many people in the bus. We have to get off somewhere but the bus is not stopping there. They tell me that as soon as the bus takes a turn, we are going to jump out. I am wondering how I can jump with my daughter in my arms. It is going to be dangerous. I am thinking about what I should do. What is the way out of this situation? It happens that the driver stops the bus and walks backwards to where I am standing. To my surprise, he turns out to be the business partner of my sister-in-law. He asks me in mild surprise, 'What are you doing here?' We then get off the bus in a deserted place surrounded by a half-built, abandoned construction.

While reflecting on his dream, the dreamer was brought face to face with an unpleasant reality: that friends and other business colleagues of his sister-in-law viewed him as an 'outsider'. This was apparent from the driver's surprised question ('What are you doing here?'). In the dream, the bus halting at an unscheduled stop and the driver walking backwards appeared to be warning signs.

While connecting the dream to reality, he began to recall a number of half-forgotten incidents and discussions with his sister-in-law that had ended in serious disagreement. An earlier business transaction had fortunately been a short-term one, and had ended-abruptly without causing serious damage. But the dream led him to seriously question the soundness of his decision. It revealed that he was about to make a big mistake—that of repeating a counter-productive pattern. It was necessary to confront this unpleasant reality and reconsider his decision, which he did in time, and with no regrets.

What is of considerable interest here from the organizational point of view is that problems discovered by the managers themselves—as frequently happens in dream workshops—are more likely to be resolved in a creative manner than the problems presented by superiors at work. Some researchers (for instance, Getzels and Csikszentmihalyi 1976) have demonstrated a strong relationship between problem identification and actual creative performance. And dream workshops can help corporations create a climate and culture that enables and motivates people to discover and solve problems independently. The discovery of such problems are nothing but 'intelligent failures' that can eventually lead to successful outcomes.

3. *Mental mobility* Mental mobility allows creative individuals to find new perspectives on and approaches to problems. Since they have a strong tendency to think in terms of opposites and unite them in inventive ways, they deal with problems through symbols using analogies and metaphors to forge new syntheses of ideas.

Mackinnon's (1971) studies recommend that in professional education, the creative potential of students can perhaps be best fostered by broadening their experience in areas that extend far beyond their specialities. He also observes that a liberal education, including the arts, humanities, social sciences and history, is much more likely to enhance self-awareness, aesthetic sensitivity and imagination than strictly professional training.

Since dreams speak in the language of metaphors, this implies an intuitive perception of similarities with the dissimilar. Gordon's (1961) research on synectics gives direct evidence of the metaphoric base of creativity. That a metaphor tends to transport us closer to a world of absolute understanding, a world more real than reality itself, was experienced by Neela, a working mother with three adult children, while working on her dream.

We are in a house. I know the people there. It is a sort of saboteurs' gang. I am there with my husband and a man and woman. The man and woman have some accomplices. They are planning to blow up this house. A thought comes to me that the house is going to be set on fire and that I must rush

out. As I go out, there is a door with curtains and two beau-
tiful turquoise earrings are stuck through them. I want to pick
them up. The woman says, 'No! No! Do not pick them up. I
will pick them up, once it is all over.'

'How silly!' I wonder. 'They are planning to blow up the
house and the earrings are going to remain there — obviously
the earrings will also be blown up!'

I then see a ship outside — not a whole one, just a skeleton.
Part of the saboteurs' gang is there. My husband points to
the ship and says, 'When the house blows up, the ship will
be damaged. So let us go and move our ship.'

At the time the dream occurred, Neela was trying to redis-
cover and establish her own identity as an artist that had been
submerged by her playing the multiple role of wife, mother and
homemaker. In addition, she was going through a painful process
of salvaging a deep, long-standing relationship with a couple who
meant a great deal to her and her husband.

In the incubation phase, she focused on the issue of establishing her identity. The quest for an identity is described by Koestler
(1964) as one of the underlying motivations of creativity.

The dream provided Neela a perspective on her 26-year-old
friendship with a couple based on a business relationship. It was
now in the process of gradually deteriorating, and both parties
had agreed to part ways and set up their own independent busi-
nesses. However, they insisted that they would continue to be
friends. Neela held the other couple responsible for sabotaging
the relationship. In her dream, the saboteurs were planning to
blow up the 'house' that had at one time been a source of comfort
and warmth to them all. Neela continued to attempt to salvage
the relationship in her dream as she did in reality by picking up
the 'beautiful turquoise earrings', using a metaphor for an orna-
mental relationship.

The dream revealed that the hollow, skeletal relationship
would get destroyed despite her efforts to salvage it. Also, her
basic assumption that the friendship would continue after the

dissolution of the business was challenged in her dream. Thus, what had happened over two years and what had been emerging in fragments in her dreams was integrated in one neat scan by her psyche.

In the dream, the dreamer uses a variety of imagery in comparing the relationship first to the house, then to the beautiful earrings, and finally to the skeleton of the ship. The ability to evoke metaphors reveals the richness and versatility of the dreamer's imagery, the potential of her mind and the possibility of developing an identity as an artist. In fact, the paradox and the beauty of the imagery helped her in creatively redirecting her thinking and developing a fresh perspective. Here, redirection involved breaking an experiential constraint and trying to salvage a dying friendship. She was simultaneously aware that her true goal was to find meaning in her own life by utilizing her time in her own creative pursuits. Thus, she discovered a new objective and course of action for herself. She was then ready to terminate a friendship that had blocked, to an extent, her creative potential. This created a natural pathway towards emotional healing; towards becoming more of what she was capable of becoming—a creative artist in her own right.

4. *To work at the edge of one's competence* As part of the creative quest, this is the ability to take risks and learn from failures. Mclelland (1963) observes that willingness to take risks is one of the key personality characteristics commonly found in creative people. Drucker (1985) has also stressed the importance of risk-taking for creativity and innovation. As Torrance (1971) points out, creative learning involves experimenting, taking risks, and making mistakes and rectifying them. Success orientation when overemphasized is detrimental to creative growth. It is often seen among managers that, even though adequately motivated, they go through a phase of 'trial and error' before they actually have a dream that offers a solution to the incubated problem. By working on the edge of his dreaming potential, where the possibility of failure lurks, the dreamer leaves himself open to greater risk of exposing a vulnerable side of himself. It requires courage to reveal oneself and share intimate feelings. The dream group creates a climate for such risk-taking, sharing of feelings and, sometimes, painful memories, that the dream group supports (Fagin 1987). Take, for instance, the dream of John D'Souza, a technical manager of a multinational company.

> *My wife and I are discussing a death in the family. A cousin from her side has expired. We go to the funeral and see the body in the coffin. The funeral procession proceeds. The dream then shifts to a later time, when my wife herself dies. This gives me a deep sense of shock. My three-year-old son is close to me. I sit on the bed and talk to my wife while she is lying down. I say, 'I love you so much. I did not mean to hurt you.' She then says, 'I wish I were with you.' At that time I become extremely emotional and I am weeping and crying when the dream ends.*

The dream revolved around the deep sense of anguish John experienced on losing his wife, whom he loved very much. She was young and beautiful, like her dead cousin in his dream. John recalled that the day before he came to the workshop they had had a violent fight over how to raise their son. After many arguments, John became so furious that he slapped his wife. While connecting the dream to the event in waking reality, for the first time he began to see that perhaps his way of dealing with people was autocratic and domineering. Unconsciously, he expected his wife to agree with him all the time—as he expected of his subordinates at work. In fact, he realized that if he continued in that attitude, he might lose her emotionally. He connected this fear with the dream image of not being able to touch her. The dream foresaw a possible problem and magnified his fear by using the powerful metaphor of death for losing her emotionally, if not physically. In reality, he harboured a tremendous sense of guilt for having hurt her. As a result, John felt that he punished himself in the dream by casting her as dead and experiencing such great sorrow.

The dream also shed light on one of his work relationships. John had received a promotion and shifted to another department. There he had to deal with an elderly subordinate who was very disgruntled and hard to work with. John tried different ways of appeasing him but always ended up in a deadlock. His incubation question, therefore, was: 'How should I deal with this elderly subordinate?' While working on this issue during the incubation session, he began to develop a different perspective on the problem. For the first time, he began to ask himself a new question: 'Am I by any chance contributing to the problem myself?'

It was clear through dreamwork that John was not defensive about his shortcomings and was therefore open to the possible need for changing his behaviour. Neither did he view his interpersonal problem at work as a threat to his self-esteem. By being courageous enough to admit to his dysfunctional behaviour, he began to actively consider the developmental factors. For instance, once he demonstrated the capability to risk self-disclosure and accept his own failure, his openness towards exploring new ways of dealing with people increased greatly. Thus, by highlighting and exposing an aspect of his behavioural pattern, this dream helped John break out of his conditioning and connect his personal and work relationships.

Needless to say, the rewards gained by working on dreams seem to far exceed the exposure involved in sharing dreams.

5. Objectivity The popular concept of creativity often highlights personal insights, flashes of illumination, and commitment. However, without objectivity the subjective world of creative people would have no reference point. Creative people not only scrutinize and judge their ideas or projects, but also actively seek advice, feedback, and criticism from colleagues to test and verify the validity of their creative solution in what Parnes (1971) calls 'deferring final judgement'. The following is the dream of a general manager of a large petroleum refining company. It is related to project work.

> *I go to a location. Perhaps it is a refinery site. I conduct the sight survey and come back to the office which, on entering, resembles a house. I have a companion, I do not remember who. I tell him to call the concerned personnel so that I can*

explain the project to them. However, I don't wait for the people to come. I am anxious, so I decide to leave. I use a stairway to go up, and an outside stairway to come down, go to my jeep and leave.

The dreamer was due for promotion. Prior to the workshop, he had given an important project proposal to the top management for approval and was anxiously awaiting sanction. He therefore had no difficulty understanding the sense of anxiety reflected in the dream. 'Will I be effective as the leader of the prestigious new project?' was one question he was at the time constantly confronted with. However, what he learned from the group's feedback about his leadership style was a revelation. He had a tendency to carry out all project responsibilities himself and faced difficulty in delegating work. This often resulted in a time gap between the commissioning and execution of the projects. That he never consulted the concerned people and discussed the tasks delegated, as reflected in the dream, was a pattern of behaviour he was not aware of. The group work offered objective feedback and evaluation of his leadership style. He realized that creative project management meant implementing new ideas and new technology and communicating effectively with and working through others involved in the project.

He also realized that although he was a seasoned technocrat, there was still room for improvement. A significant outcome of the process was the creative shift of the manager from his earlier conformity to traditional perceptions, which focus only on task orientation, to a flexible and adaptable attitude in dealing with the process of managing change.

Thus, dreams often highlight a pattern of behaviour in the dreamer that needs change, while dreamwork facilitates the process of pattern recognition (also acknowledged by Krippner and Dillard 1988). This leads to the development of a broader behavioural repertoire, which enables managers to function effectively in a variety of situations. The input of behavioural learning through dreamwork, for example, is in many ways as relevant to managers today as the technical and material concerns facing them.

6. *Motivation* Behind all creative efforts is intrinsic motivation. Creative people are involved in enterprise for its own sake, and not necessarily for reward. They are self-driven, attracted by the challenge the problem or enterprise presents. Repucci's (1971) and Amabile and Grysklewicz's (1988) studies confirm selfmotivation as a personal stimulant and an intrinsic principle of creativity.

Mr Khanna, a senior manager of a petroleum company, narrated a recurring dream in the workshop.

> *I am with my family members and we are walking in a shopping complex which is awfully crowded. My youngest daughter, initially alongside us, is walking fast and far ahead of the rest of us. I call out her name loudly, 'Anita . . . Anita,' but she does not respond. In the process, my wife and elder daughter are left behind. There is considerable distance between the three subgroups, and that makes me very uncomfortable. After a few moments a funny thing happens. My elder daughter starts clapping behind me, to which I respond. This goes on for a long time.*

Mr Khanna had this dream when he was expecting to be transferred to another city. After a long period of separations, the family (consisting of his wife and two daughters) would be able to stay together during this tenure for the first time in years. Earlier, due to frequent transfers Mr Khanna had had to move his family to his hometown because of inadequate educational facilities in the places he was posted to. This arrangement was satisfactory in terms of the children's education, but deprived him of family contact and togetherness for long stretches. However, he was very distressed when he discovered that his younger teenage daughter was growing up in a manner quite contrary to his expectations, with interests and inclinations which he, as a father, was unable to appreciate or encourage. She was becoming somewhat alienated, distancing herself from the rest of the family. Since he had not dealt with his growing feeling of uneasiness directly, his anxiety worsened at the prospect of the impending transfer. He had frequent visions of losing touch with his daughter entirely if she were to stay behind in hostel to complete her graduation. This was at the back of his mind when he came to the workshop.

It was necessary to work through his anxiety and sense of failure as a father and to explore ways of establishing new links with her as he could so easily with his elder daughter. Separation from his grown children seemed to touch on an old issue of his separation from his own parents that had not yet been resolved. Its emergence in the dream helped Mr Khanna to realize the fact. As Ullman (1979) puts it: 'Enhanced self-awareness rather than magical resolution of problems is the end product of effective dreamwork.'

A follow-up indicated that the dreamer communicated his dream insights to his family members following a crucial change in attitude. The feeling of anxiety was finally dispelled and the dream ceased to recur. Even now, after many years, the dreamer acknowledges the experience of that particular dream group as one of the most powerful and memorable experiences of his life.

Dreamwork means different things to different people. For some it is a tool for enhancing self-awareness; for others it heightens problem-solving abilities; for yet others it suggests a direct link with diverse forms of self-empowerment—a fascinating link that has been largely unexplored.

SEVEN

The Royal Road to Empowerment

WHILE DRIVING FROM downtown Washington to the airport a couple of years ago, the friendly cab-driver asked me, 'How does corporate India treat a woman manager?' He proceeded to provide a context to his question by narrating a story about his sister, an administrative manager in a multinational company.

'One day, back in the late 1980s, when my sister Karen was in her office, a young man walked in and stood in front of her. Looking directly at her, he asked, "I have a crisis coming up. Do you think you can manage it on behalf of your company?"'

Despite having worked for several years and in various positions of authority, Karen realized that her struggle with the stereotype of women as lacking competence and the abilities of leadership and crisis management was far from over.

'Of course, this was a long time ago. But have times since changed for women?' he asked me.

'Yes and no. Women experience a sense of hope on joining the workforce and look forward to a "fulfilling" employment and not merely "full-time" employment. Since women's entry into the business world is a recent phenomenon, there are difficulties in coming to terms with it,' I said, watching the fast-moving landscape of colourful tulips and avenues of dogwood trees then in full blossom.

Pathway to power

It is often felt that women have not been successful up to now in holding positions of power and authority because, psychologically speaking, they have been conditioned to locate the centre of authority outside of themselves: in their fathers and brothers while growing up and in their husbands' after marriage. Holding organizational authority demands a conscious effort to create that power centre within oneself.

How does the power centre relate to what women do at work? Clearly, the freedom to perform a range of functions at work is the first step on the pathway to power. In empowering jobs, there is a chance to invent, plan, create, design and improve. The higher the component of established routine and procedure, the more powerless one feels. Power goes to the path-breaker, the explorer of new territory, the first in the new function rather than the one who follows. It requires 'inner work' together with the conscious decision to gradually shift from the 'pleasing' mode to the 'influencing' mode. As Gloria Steinem (1992) says, this power needs to be redefined not as domination but as self-determination and self-esteem.

This leads us to an understanding of why women are seen more in areas which are an extension of their 'housekeeper' role, for instance, public relations, personnel and administration, which until recently were not power centres in terms of the critical contingencies of organizations. One can discern institutional patterns of women being tracked into 'powerless' jobs, that is, those entailing less flexibility, more routine, greater orientation towards maintenance than innovation, less visibility, and often no relevance to critical problem-solving. Therefore, to feel empowered in a job, women need to engage themselves in activities relevant to organizations' critical contingencies and to their own visibility. Lacking these characteristics—freedom, relevance, visibility—together we can begin to understand why women tend to identify with the male model of managerial success as they move up the carrier path. It becomes so crucial in order to survive in male-dominated organizations that they end up rejecting even the valued feminine traits such as sensitivity, self-reflective thinking, interdependence, empathy, collaboration and nurturance that they might have earlier possessed. The argument here is not for keeping women in solely nurturant, expressive and communicative roles; rather, it is for building upon these qualities as strengths rather than denying their value because they do not fit into hierarchical organization.

To hold on to the values that one feels are important while simultaneously working in organizations that uphold other values can be quite tough. Because this can make them personally vulnerable, prove ineffective in competitive environments, and limit their chances of promotion, as these are antithetical to the competitive, independent achievement-oriented model they see round them. From the organizational point of view, those in power (who are mostly men), encourage, advance and mentor mostly men, but rarely women. Not surprisingly, then, the handful of women who actually manage to rise high in organizations usually resemble men in terms of power.

Awakening the feminine

In 1990, some of us, representing Indian public sector enterprises, founded the Forum for Women in Public Sector, which is committed to the growth and development of women. The Forum focuses attention on the invisible priorities of working women by promoting equality in gender issues through a variety of concrete programmes.

External barriers—in terms of social or organizational constraints—are generally considered severe impediments in women's development. While working on these barriers through a specially designed programme, it emerged that there are several internal barriers too. In fact, the self-imposed internal barriers are more difficult to recognize and accept, and therefore more difficult to overcome. These are the barriers that are created very early in life and hence become a tenacious part of oneself.

It is as if the feminine potential has been discounted, neglected and restricted for so long that it has remained so even in cases where the barriers have ceased to exit. This is true not only for women who are underprivileged or doubly discriminated against, but even for supposedly privileged and powerful women. Despite holding positions of power these women leave behind a central core of themselves when they enter the corporate world. However, they carry the burden of their self-imposed barriers such as self-doubt, and lack of self-esteem, realistic self-appraisal and self-confidence, which prevents them from striving for success in general and effectively dealing with personal and organizational issues in particular. This is so despite the fact that crosscultural studies show no evidence of gender affecting achievement motivation, risk-taking, task perseverance or other related skills (Schwartz 1990). This inspired me to design and conduct custom-made management development programmes to deal with the issues of stereotyping, identity, power and authority.

For women executives, these programmes are a platform for experience sharing and critical questioning about how to balance career and family. Although an effective catharsis, this does not create real-time change. Their feeling of powerlessness comes from being peripheral to problem-solving and change-creating actions, which they would like to be integral to. However, this experience itself starts a process of introspection, because the programme offers an opportunity to women to suspend their day-to-day preoccupations and reconsider why they are doing what they are doing from a fresh perspective. It is therefore not unusual that a couple of days later some participants report having had powerful dreams, which need careful appreciation.

For many women, these programmes became an avenue to dreamwork, inspiring them to explore dreams for a deeper understanding of their identity as women. When we are in a crisis or in a state of transition, dreams bring messages from a deeper level of consciousness, thus providing a source of reorientation to a new state of consciousness. In some cases, they also help in finding new directions. Eventually it was dreamwork that resolved certain deep existential issues that had surfaced during the management development programmes.

The frequency of such occurrences led me to design dream workshops in order to address specific needs of women in employment. After several such workshops it can be argued that dreamwork is a highly effective source of empowerment. And empowerment here implies exercising options and choices about one's life and work, influencing and mobilizing people and eliciting their co-operation, and playing a crucial role in decision-making.

Speaking in a different voice

It is often said that women possess far greater ease of communication than men. But do women know how to value their own experiences, believe in their own values and listen to their own inner voices? Do they know how to speak 'in a different voice' in order to be heard? What happens when the communication channels are blocked? These issues bring to mind the dream of a programme director at the television centre in Bombay.

> *I am in a posh, sprawling, white house. Apparently, that house belongs to the federal government and for the first time it has been opened to public. I am keen to see the house from inside. It has antique furniture and beautiful carpets. It has been done up tastefully. I have a friendly boy with me. I met him there; I did not know him earlier. Curious, we both go upstairs. The top floor is totally disappointing considering the efforts we make to get there. There is nothing much to see there. In the meantime, it somehow gets dark and the boy disappears. I lose my way and am terribly frightened. I scream for help but it seems people do not hear me.*

After we explored all the images of the dream it became clear that as a single working woman the dreamer was most concerned about the fact that she was not 'settled'. She was getting increasingly worried about her advancing age and single status. Further, the dream also illuminated the fact that she was fast losing contact with the sunny, carefree, 'friendly' part of herself. Her own nature had become an enigma to her. She had become uncommunicative and withdrawn. She kept to herself at the office, feeling dejected, and hardly ever mixed with friends. This shift in behaviour at the workplace created stress because her job demanded dealing with people and effectively communicating with them. She became agonizingly aware that she would be relegating herself to a lonesome existence for the rest of her life if she continued that way. The investment she had made in gradually reaching the top of her profession seemed as empty as the top floor of the white house.

And with that realization, emotions from the past began to flood into the present with familiar feelings of hopelessness and despair. These feelings then became a lever to retrieve suppressed, traumatic episodes at work, episodes too painful to deal with on her own. They had left her with a negative self-image and low self-esteem, mainly because she was expected to be subservient. She coped with this in the only way possible: by withdrawing into herself. The coldness, especially towards herself, and towards others, put out her creative fire and inhibited her creative abilities.

The dream had a tremendous impact on her. She later told me that the strain of catharsis was too much for her. As a result, she spent a week in bed, partly reflecting, partly taking courage to face the unpleasant aspects of herself, and partly coming to terms with it. This eventually led to a dramatic change in her life. She made heroic efforts to break out of the pattern: she picked up the old hobbies and interests she had abandoned, and took up professional courses that would enrich her professional life. She eventually fell in love, got married to the man of her choice and now enjoys a happy married life.

Confronting issues of security

Dreams often reflect an interplay among unresolved personal issues that mirror unresolved tension in society. Women often complain about unfair practices, and unequal distribution of resources or simply counter-productive attitudes that are firmly institutionalized. These make them feel as 'second-class citizens'. Then, there are issues of security, safety and protection that are crucial to women's development as well as empowerment. These often come up in dreams. For instance, an architect in the town-planning department of the state administration had the following dream:

> *I am somewhere in the bush, perhaps in Africa, in a camper (a camping mobile) and my husband and his photographic partner are in the sleeping bags behind the vehicle. I see some lions coming out of the bush and loping behind where we have kept the supplies. While I am safe in the camper, a part of me wants to tell my husband 'Don't forget to watch out for the lions.'*

In outlining the dream, the dreamer spoke about her marital discord. She was not too sure that she had reason enough to stay married. However, there was the issue of security. Also, she had recently found out that she was suffering from an ailment that required long-term medical treatment. At that point of time this made security more important and movement less so. Yet, there was also a conscious effort to gradually move from the protection of her husband to that of herself, as depicted by the mobile in the dream. She was particularly pleased to note that although her place traditionally was beside her husband, she was not there any longer. Connecting the dream to reality, she also stated that the photographic partner in the dream had in fact been emerging as her husband's soulmate in recent times since they both shared similar interests and spent a lot of time together in common pursuits. Hence, she felt lonely and isolated most of the time.

The camper was a metaphor for protection, for assurance of comfort. At that point of time she also needed to shield herself from certain colleagues who she described as strong, proud, intimidating and basically lazy like the feline creatures in her dream. These colleagues were trying to lobby against one of the projects earlier approved by the Board by taking advantage of the fact that the company had a new board of directors. They had attacked a particular project proposal in one of the board meetings without much success. However, she continued to feel isolated at work.

After sharing her concerns and dilemma regarding the issues

connected with the dream, she also wondered why someone like her—assertive, competent, economically independent and free of responsibilities—need worry about giving up the traditional role and feel helpless and insecure. Clearly, the transition from being a woman to being a person and a professional would require taking a stand on one's personal values and convictions. But working on her dream helped her recognize and reinforce some of her personal values and convictions and feel stronger and more positive about the future. Although there were many issues to be resolved, the dreamer began to feel empowered enough to deal with them in due course of time.

The emerging signature of the self

Described here is a dream of an administrative manager of a large manufacturing company. The dreamer is in her mid-thirties, a widow with two children.

> I am going up in a lift to the top floor of a high-rise building. My boss is there with me. On the top floor, I step out of the lift and come down a floor by the staircase. On the terrace of this floor I notice that a very big tree has grown through the concrete of the building and reached the top.

> There are no cracks in the cement floor but a clean-cut hole, as if it is the most natural thing to happen. I wonder how this lush green, tender tree could survive the cold, harsh concrete and grow to its full potential, reach the top floor and grow even further.

At the time the dream occurred the dreamer was grappling with the dilemma of balancing her professional role and the role of a widowed daughter-in-law of a Hindu joint family. The family was politically prominent, and had a conventional lifestyle and simple living habits but expected the women to remain within the four walls of the house. However, the dreamer was permitted to work outside the house in order to earn a livelihood. Not content with her limited role, she secretly nursed the ambition of joining active politics. Despite her economic independence, she continued to feel powerless and invisible, as if her true worth had not been recognized. But she could not muster the courage to talk openly about her aspirations for fear of opposition and ridicule from her 'very powerful' brothers-in-law. This conflict evoked feelings of confusion, anger and resentment within her. The continued ambivalence towards the need to assert herself and the fear of disapproval from others left her feeling torn.

The dreamer was gently led back to the experience of the dream. A thorough investigation of all the images in the dream was conducted. The tree in the dream symbolized for the dreamer her own life-force and creative energy. Sensing that this image with strong emotional overtones would unravel many underlying themes, the dreamer was asked to describe the tree in greater detail.

It turned out that the tree in question was a *neem* (margosa) tree, a tree of all seasons, known for its medicinal value and numerous other uses. The dreamer wryly mentioned that except for the fact that its fruit is bitter, all other parts of the tree are quite useful. The description of the tree resonated with her personality.

The dreamer felt that she was always ready to give her resources to her family and actively rendered support in important family matters. Her grievance, however, was that despite the fact that she could be relied upon in times of crisis, she was conveniently forgotten once the crisis was over. Her competence was viewed as a threat to the traditional women of the house, a 'bitter' truth that had to be swallowed but not to be approved of.

The image of the tree as a metaphor for herself was so powerful that it had a transforming effect. It worked on her mind, on her thinking and imagination. For the first time now it struck her that it was possible to harness one's potential without causing a split in the family. The tender tree with its vibrant life-force and energy had been able to pierce even through the hard concrete in order to reach the top. This insight released the tremendous energy that had until then remained suppressed within her.

The dreamwork apparently exposed the dreamer to more about herself than she was ready to handle at the time, input that touched her at many levels of her psyche. Her insights at that point were several, but the deepest one was that she had reached a threshold where, as Joseph Campbell describes it, 'the old concept, ideals and emotional meaning no longer fit'. It seemed to her that she could no longer conform to her old identity; what had once felt secure now felt life-denying.

A few months later the dreamwork inspired the dreamer to take courage and join the political party of her choice. She has not looked back since. She has actively participated in conducting meetings, addressing rallies, and in schemes for the welfare of women. She has thus created a new role and new space for herself. To her amazement, the dreamer also discovered a new-found respect and dignity at home.

It is a common observation that women tend to devote time to the crises of others but neglect to create a relationship with their own innermost aspirations and desires. But like all relationships of value, this relationship too demands time, space and nurturing, otherwise it can cause stress and anxiety in the daily life of a woman, making her use enormous energy for the simplest of chores.

Creating new equations

I am sitting in the back seat of a black car full of people and the car takes a turn to the right on a rough road. There is a familiar feeling of pleasure as my eyes feast on my 'dream house'. There it is on the corner plot of that turn, a garden of yellow, pink and orange flowers in flower beds, leading up to a solid grey granite house. In the first floor corridor there is a white railing. Over the railing drapes an orange bougainvillea. Prominently in the background of the first floor corridor are beautiful green palms with yellow spiked tips. Every

*day I pass this delightful, lovely house and feast my eyes
with pleasure on the flowers and every day I remember
catching my breath when my eyes rest on the palms. These
palms always create a sense of disturbance.*

*The scene then shifts to running down a wide tar highway.
I am running away in terror from a man in a red-and-blue
checked shirt and blue jeans. He is almost upon me, with
his hands outstretched to catch me. I stop to stand with
the man at the corner of the 'house'. I feel tranquillity and
peace. I wait with him till my pursuer races past. I then
slowly begin to relax.*

The dreamer, a Christian with two teenaged sons and separated
from her husband for the past nine years, was a manager in a five-
star deluxe hotel. Despite the long separation, her parents had
been continuing to force her to go back to her husband, whose
only qualification was his affluence. However, the dreamer refused
to go back to the confining relationship she had left behind.

At the time the dream occurred, there were two men in the
dreamer's life. One was attractive, exciting, though selfish and
demanding; a disturbing fact she preferred to ignore. This is not
surprising because we often develop certain attitudes and suppress
the feelings that are at variance with them. The other was a stable,
secure, man—a friend not only to her but also to her sons, a fact
she took for granted. These simultaneous relationships created
tension and conflict. The dreamer felt that she was sinking deep
into the swamp of confusion and uncertainty.

This is when the dream came to her rescue. It focused on the
relationships and highlighted the 'emotional sore spot' she had
not known existed. This became clear when we began to explore
the metaphors of the dream. Her association with the dream
image of 'the attractive palms with yellow spiked tips' eventually
led her to recognize a similar feeling of discomfort and alarm that
her friend often evoked in her. A spark of understanding flashed
when there was a felt sense of connection between the dream
image of the 'attractive palms' and the waking reality of her
pursuer. She wondered: 'How did I manage not to see what was

so obvious? How could I ever think of marrying someone who created disturbance and tension at a deeper level?' She felt certain that he would never have accepted her and her two sons as part of his family. The dream cut through the pretension and delusion of waking life and brought the dreamer face to face with her real problem.

It is interesting to note how dreams help us by their ruthless honesty. In fact, dreams cannot thrive in an atmosphere of enforced 'political or business correctness' or by being thrust into old, burnt-out paradigms. They thrive on fresh perceptions, honesty and self-integrity.

At that time, the dreamer decided to do first things first, that is, act on her decision to put an end to this disturbing relationship, whatever might be the outcome.

Despite this conscious resolve, it took her nearly two months to muster enough courage and strength to make the final break. The other man was a pillar of support and helped her overcome the anguish of the broken relationship. He also gently helped her restore her lost equilibrium. It is then that she began to see him in a new light.

Two years later I received acknowledgement of the dreamwork I had done earlier. In a letter the dreamer recounted how she had succeeded in creating a new equation with her other friend, whom she described as a solid and secure man, and how happy she was after marrying him.

In an unprecedented gesture, she also offered her 'dream material' as a resource for others. She expressed the hope that it might inspire others to cross confining thresholds and make new beginnings.

Recognizing the predicament

In a dream workshop exclusively organized for the women managers of a state-owned multi-unit manufacturing corporation, a training manager recounted the following dream:

*I see myself getting up in the middle of the night wanting
to go to the toilet. I open the door. The water tank over the
commode has come off its hinges. The hook is broken. As
soon as I step in, the tank explodes. There is water all over
the floor. I feel shattered. In the dream I curse myself for not
getting the damn thing repaired in time.*

The group work on the dream brought out the dreamer's preoc-
cupation with her state of chronic procrastination. Although she
was aware of the fact that the facility needed urgent repair, she
drifted passively along in her daily routine and pretended to
herself that she had not noticed the broken toilet. She was also
aware that the problem might worsen if she continued to neglect
it, and render the facility completely dysfunctional.

The dreamer was easily able to connect the dream to her working situation as well. She confessed that she had been feeling
outshined and outperformed at work for over a year by people
whom she called 'non-performers'. She had not done much
about the predicament although she was acutely aware of it and
strongly felt that she needed to act. This pattern was also reflected
in personal relationships, where she felt pushed around, cramped
and taken for granted.

As depicted in the dream, her predicament revolved around the
dilemma of whether to use an active coping strategy or a passive
one. This entrenched pattern of behaviour was highlighted in
the dream and she became agonizingly conscious of it—as never
before. Someone in the group saw the image of an exploded
tank as a 'warning' that things would get out of hand if she
continued to play unconscious about important things in life.
She would continue to feel 'overwhelmed' by people, events
and situations and get acted upon by them. The pattern of
surrendering one's core life might have begun in early childhood,
but until one is forced to take a fresh look at it—as dreams often
challenge us to do—one may be exceedingly vulnerable to being
overwhelmed by the needs of others. A dream such as this also
shows that the dreamer's life needs to change, that she has got
trapped in a dysfunctional pattern, that she is afraid to take the

next step, to claim her own power and resources for being and acting, and for working to full capacity.

Although the process of dreamwork helps clarify the confusion related to a problem in the mind of the dreamer, in waking life its confusion remains far from being resolved for a variety of reasons. It is fatuous to think that once we gain clarity about an issue the confusion dissipates, that once we resolve an issue it remains resolved forever, or once we learn about important matters in life we remain conscious and alert ever after. No matter how many times we go through such learnings, there are more 'first times' awaiting us.

The real excitement of learning through dreams is that dreams continue to bring us letters from our unconscious before we are sometimes even ready to read them, before we feel that we are strong enough to deal with them. We respond to dreams before we know how to speak the language, before we know exactly whom we are speaking to, before the feelings are even 'speech ripe'.

The dreams of women managers are of interest for several reasons. First, they underline the fact that working women are passing through a period of transition. Although the corporate role gives them economic independence and a certain amount of visibility, its expectations are more confining than liberating. It takes a great deal of determination and strength to break free primarily because the cultural and social systems provide little or no support to deal with these crucial existential aspects of tradition-bound roles. For women, the professional and family roles are simultaneous, not sequential as Hall (1972) observes is the case of men. Men can wear their family-role hats only in the evening after work, whereas women's family-role hat—invisible as it may be between 9 and 5—is simply never taken off. It appears that this pattern of professional development is superimposed on the existing social system without much modification. As a result, there is a gap between the two systems, which continue to generate pressures from within.

Also, the perceived dichotomy between the Western corporate

culture that prevails in the topsoil of Indian business and industry and the Indian values and traditions that form its subsoil makes deep psychological exploration quite an overwhelming exercise. However, it is remarkable how the process of dreamwork has enabled women executives to raise questions about their deepest concerns and challenge old patterns of the most private aspects of their life in the public sphere of the dream group. Clearly, dreamwork helps dreamers identify and prioritize their problems and empower them to take major decisions in their lives.

Second, it is my firm belief that dreamwork when compared to other management development programmes has the distinct advantage of 'fast-forwarding' change because it gives the dreamer an opportunity to engage in a critique of everyday life involving the 'whole' person, that is, attitudes, experiences and values. This leads to the profound realization that dreams actually present to the dreamer a cross-section of his self. The images that arise from the core have the power to change in a manner that is difficult to accomplish by logic, reason or will alone. This realization can lead to the growth of the power potential in women, enabling them to make a shift from passivity and powerlessness to dignity, distinction and empowerment. After conducting dream workshops as well as regular management development programmes, this view has crystallized. Further, Winter's (1973) studies confirm that men and women with a high degree of power motivation are also able to recall their dreams more often.

Third, the potency of dreamwork is such that it releases the energy that has been suppressed and unblocks creative potential. According to Perls (1969), the father of Gestalt therapy, who used a specialized form of role-plying technique:

> All the different parts of the dream are fragments of our personalities. Since our aim is to make every one of us a wholesome person, which means a unified person, without conflicts what we have to do is put the different fragments of the dream together. We have to re-own these projected, fragmented parts of our personality and re-own the hidden potential that appears in the dream.

The emergence of the opposite

It is amazing how dreamers find themselves responding positively to the content and feelings generated by dreams, no matter how upsetting or disturbing they are in the beginning. In this process, a range of emotions, from spoken resentments to feelings of affection, often come to the surface, where they can be understood or resolved. It is fascinating to see how the process of dreamwork by focusing on the rejected parts as reflected in dreams, awakens the latent dimensions of a dreamer's personality. This leads to a reconciling of conflicting aspects and hence restoration of equilibrium.

For instance, women managers who are given to personalizing every event and situation in the workplace from the victimized, depressed, persecuted 'why me?' mode, learn to depersonalize, and distance themselves from those. This grants them the freedom to move from attachment to separation, from a diffused to a differentiated identity, within established work relationships. This perspective gradually enables them to own up their strength and self-worth. They no longer need permission to be themselves. The emergence of the self is equally imperative to establishing one's true identity, with which comes the realization that the art of living lies in learning from what happens to us, not in trying to control it.

The situation is diametrically opposite in the case of male managers. Their attitudes often mellow during the course of dreamwork: power-based statements get tempered by a profound undercurrent of humanism, care and concern; tales of victories take on a realistic hue. It is amazing how those who are initially reticent or those who are reluctant to express their feelings for fear of being judged as weak and emotional, not only find their voice but also connect with profound emotions. Those facile with words discover a more authentic source to speak from.

Here, several instances come to mind. A computer engineer once shared a dream in the group. Thereafter, he became very reticent, as if the 'sharing' itself had been too much. Hence, no headway could be made, as he withdrew into himself. He was not forthcoming with any information regarding the context of the dream either. However, inexplicably, the projection of feelings on the dream in the first phase of experiential dreamwork touched him. He subsequently admitted that the empathy and concern of the group members had encouraged him to open up and articulate his real concern. He confessed his deep anguish over the dying relationship between himself and his wife despite his love for her. The group gave a candid feedback about how difficult it had been for them to reach him. As a consequence, he decided that he would make fresh efforts to bridge the communication gap between him and his wife.

Indeed, both men and women are capable of the full range of behaviour and both men and women need to liberate themselves from the polarities of gender that force them into limited and limiting roles. Dreaming is a quest for wholeness. It does not demand that the dreamer abandon traditional behaviour, whether masculine or feminine; it calls for blending each with its opposite. By learning the language of emotions through dreams, effective managers of the future, will be able to combine competence with compassion and reason with intuition.

EIGHT

Dreams of the Future and the Future of Dreams

S OMETIMES WE do things without knowing why we are doing them. For instance, in July 1994 I went to Holland. Apparently, I went there for the International Conference on Dreams, then on to Switzerland—the wonderland which bears the signature of one of the greatest dream masters of all time—for more work on dreams. Frankly, I did not know then what made me go there at that point of time when I should have stayed put and invested more into my professional life that was rapidly losing all meaning for me.

I found myself at a crossroads. Which road should I take? The left was a widely travelled one with familiar landmarks and other professionals as companions. The one going right was not really a road. One had to create one's own path. I was note sure whether I would survive on that one. Yet, whenever I thought that I should leave dreamwork, something within me would cry out in tune with the Gnostic gospels: 'If you bring forth what is within you, what you bring forth will save you. If you do not bring forth what is within you what you do not bring forth will destroy you.'

Little wonder then that in 'that land of dreams', I had the dream of my life.

I am riding a bicycle in the twilight in an easy and effortless way. Dusk has fallen. Riding along a road I come upon a

*rectangular plot of land to my right, where I know I am
going to build my new home. It is quite a lot of land. There
is a small shrine right in the centre of the plot. I take a close
look. Aha! It turns out to be a* shivalingam. *I wonder how
I can possibly construct my home with the shrine in the
centre. This would require displacing it from its original
place for the sake of having more space for construction.
I feel terrible at the thought. I would rather build my new
home around it. Yes, I want to make it an integral part of my
new home.*

It was a dream that left me with a special feeling that stayed
with me for several days. In fact, I make powerful, important
connections to it even now. I am also grateful for the exquisite manner in which its significance was revealed to me by Dr
Theodore Abt, professor of agronomy and economic planning at
the Federal Institute of Technology and a training analyst at the
C.G. Jung Institute in Zurich, who, sensing my anguish, acted
like a natural healer. Working on the series of dreams connected
with this issue, he integrated all that was fragmented within me.

The visual quality of the dream was such that it gave me
solace beyond words. At that point of time, I had all kinds of
doubts about the survival of dreamwork as an alternative model
of executive education. I would often wonder whether this 'soft'
technique for dealing with 'hard' problems would be criticized
or ridiculed by management professionals. Although right from
the beginning there had been more requests to conduct dream
workshops for organizations across the country than I could
possibly handle with my full-time job, I remained totally divided
and fragmented over this issue. Should I give up my regular job
and take up dreamwork on a full-time basis?

Light upon the unlit shore

Let me here share my experience of an unexpected meeting with
Dr Marie Louis von Franz, a psychoanalyst based in Bollingen,
Switzerland, and a close associate of C.G. Jung. I had heard that

she does not see visitors because she keeps indifferent health and tires easily. But having come this far, with a friend who had a prior appointment with her, I felt that I just had to meet her.

Dr von Franz's house, a tower-like structure, is located in the countryside, surrounded by woods. I reached there, uncertain about whether or not I would be able to meet her. While I waited, I watched the sun's rays shimmering in a nearby pond, a water-snake rise to the surface and go in again. The timeless quality of the forest, dense with trees, fragrant with water, had a strange and quietening influence on me. I wandered around keeping my fingers crossed.

How should I break through the invisible ring around the tower? The forest was unusually silent.

Just then, as if on cue, the front door opened and my friend called me in to meet Dr von Franz. She was sitting at the head of the table, body slightly bent, blue eyes focused, face radiant.

'I am delighted to be able to see you. As if . . . as if . . . a dream has come true,' I said.

'A dream? To see an old crone?' she asked modestly.

'No, no, I see a radiant being,' I heard myself saying.

'How long will you be here?' she asked me.

'Just a couple of days,' I said, suddenly feeling a bit sad. It is strange how one sometimes connects to a certain place and time with a special feeling.

'Really? Then you must come again to study Switzerland,' she said, almost echoing my own feelings.

To study Switzerland?

For a moment, I reflected back on my few days in Zurich— to the swim in the lake that had felt almost therapeutic; to the beauty of Chagall's chancel-stained windows; to the rejuvenating quality of the landscape. How soothing it had all been to my tortured soul experiencing its 'dark night' then.

An old memory from another time, another place was stirred and brought back to life. Back in India, en route to the drilling camp in the oil fields in the hinterland of Rajasthan, at the end of a hot and grueling field day, I had once chanced upon the octagonal sun temple near Dilwara. A site of beauty and serenity but with no deity, its inner sanctum filled with the golden light of the setting sun, as though an invocation to one's own innate greatness.

The palpable energy of that sacred site had been refreshing and energizing in a strangely similar way.

'Most certainly, if Switzerland also wants it to happen that way,' I said.

We then talked about the forthcoming conference, 'Dreaming in India', part of a series across the globe: 'Dreaming in Russia', 'Dreaming in Greece' and 'Dreaming in India'. Initiated by the Jungian psychoanalyst Robert Bosnak, this series had the objectives of bringing the international dreamworker community together in order to revitalize dreamwork and to study the foremost collective dreams of that location and incubate new dreams. For example, in the case of 'Dreaming in Russia'—which took place during the August revolution in 1991—had as its theme resistance to oppression; 'Dreaming in Greece' in 1993 was about democracy; and 'Dreaming in India' was centred around non-violence. These conferences focus on the themes to such an extent that dreams on these get naturally incubated, and subsequently shared and worked with on a collective level.

But what is the relationship among dreams, imagination, social action and responsibility? Usually, cultural differences and competitive goals initially prevent us from coming together, in dream groups or otherwise. Often, it is when some emotional or spiritual insight manages to break through—as often happens in dream groups—that the differences seem to transcend the divides.

Mary Watkins (1992) points out that in recent years there has been a trend to concentrate on images that heal stress, insecurity, etc., and increase personal power and enhance personal growth. Similarly, concentrating on images of breaking down the barriers between one nation and another could become instrumental in promoting peace. In this context, dreamwork might prove to be one of the best ways of creating a strong sense of community within heterogeneous groups.

'That is very well, but you must also get real dreams to study,' Dr von Franz insisted, bringing me back to the given moment.

'Could you please give a message for the conference?' I requested, feeling a strange right over her. After all, dreams connect people across the globe.

'I cannot think it now. Maybe later . . . I will improvise something.' After a pause she said, 'When you go back, read the Upanishads. Read them with naïveté. Then, maybe then, you can avoid being poisoned by any particular style of thinking.'

And then, suddenly, out of nowhere, one of my long-buried dreams was resurrected.

I am in transit at an international airport. I walk up to an information counter where a Western middle-aged lady is standing in front of a tree-shaped pillar. The pillar is extraordinarily beautiful, made of silver and exuding light. 'Do you know how to get to a place where ancient dream incubation [a la C.A. Meir the author of the book on dream incubation] is still practised?' I ask her.

'I will not take you there. But you will have to take your own WMC to get there,' my dream-lady replies.

Let me here tell you that WMC was the number of one of my old cars and that the lady in the dream reminds me of a friend, a Russian Jew settled in San Francisco, now a Buddhist practising eastern techniques of meditation—a multifaceted identity.

The dream clearly tells me to take myself, my ideas, my work far more seriously than I have so far. The dream also encourages me to have more faith in myself and my professional intuition to follow certain interesting but unexplored leads on the ancient approaches to dream yoga.

I then remembered several dreams from my past that had urged me into studying Eastern approaches to dream yoga. Dreams that I had not thought about in a long time.

The sudden sparking of interest in late 1994 in the Eastern heritage of dreaming took me on an impulse to the Tibetan monasteries in the East. There I found encouraging leads that opened up new perspectives before me. For instance, I had an enlightening discussion with the Venerable Tokchok, a lama of

rare sensitivity and inward poise, of the Chorten monastery at
Gangtok. Although he took me on a guided tour of the monastery, it was difficult to strike a conversation with him until I
accidentally broached the subject of dreaming—accidentally for
him, not for me.

Referring to the Tibetan texts, the Venerable Tokchok gave an
elaborate classification of dreams based on the five elements in
the human constitution: earth, air, water, fire, and ether or sky.
In ancient times it was believed that the predominance of one
element in the human constitution could trigger certain kinds
of dreams. In fact, certain pathological disorders in people could
be attributed to the predominance of a given constitutional
element, much like Hippocrates spoke of four classical temper-
aments (choleric, phlegmatic, melancholic, sanguine) and the
contemporary psychologist Sheldon associated body types with
certain personality characteristics. One can therefore argue that
the expression 'to be in one's element' might suggest just the right
balance between the elements in the body and one's state of mind.

Then, His Eminence Venerable Tai Situ Rimpoche, head of
the ancient Roomtek monastery, spoke at length on dreaming
and stated that it is part of a secret doctrine.

> A dream is as real while you are dreaming as is reality while you are
> awake. If you practise devotion during the day you will dream of
> devotion during the night. If you practise compassion during the
> day you will dream of compassion during the night. In fact one
> has to practise it so well that even in a dream the practise does not
> get disturbed. As you are dreaming a dream of being a woman,
> similarly he is [pointing to a devotee in the room] dreaming a
> dream of being a man. But you must remember that you are a
> Buddha [an enlightened one] just as he is a Buddha too. We there-
> fore don't pay much attention to dreams beyond a point.

I was struck by the paradoxical value system within the same
culture. On the one hand, elaborate attention is given to dreams
to enhance the understanding of a particular state of consciousness, and on the other an effort is made to transcend the very
state of consciousness in order to attain the state of deep sleep,
during which dreaming also ceases and what remains is the most
comprehensive, unwavering consciousness.

Given this context, the words of Dr von Franz took on a special sense of urgency and intensity. I saw my dreams being reborn with a new sense of vitality, a new sense of direction. Something fell into place.

'I am very grateful for this meeting, Dr von Franz,' I said with feeling.

'This must be the magic of India,' she said.

'Really? I thought it was the other way round.' I then briefly reflected on how I had seriously contemplated ways of breaking through what I thought was an invisible ring protecting her house.

She nodded, with a twinkle in her eyes and a hint of a smile, and simply said, 'Now, you see!'

We all had a hearty laugh and felt profoundly connected.

And, suddenly, there was light on the unlit shore of my consciousness. I wondered why the work that had earlier seemed secure and comforting now felt so stifling and life-denying. I felt I could not longer confine myself to that sort of one-dimensional professional identity anymore. How could I find ways to integrate the old pattern with the new? The dream came up with an answer, an answer of a different kind.

The spontaneous appearance of a *shivalingam* in my dream—even though I am not particularly influenced by any religious tradition—had a tremendously positive effect on me. In Hindu mythology the *shivalingam* is a symbol of the union of Shakti and Shiva, the supreme androgyny, the sacred marriage of the male and female principles, the universal source of creativity. In the Hindu trinity of creation, regeneration and destruction, Shiva is the god of creative destruction, which signifies the end of the old order and the beginning of the new.

The union of opposites symbolized by the *shivalingam* signified the emergence of my new (professional) being; the foundation of a new profession for me that would be built around dreamwork. At this point, I realized that integrating dreamwork and management would lead to a new and holistic model of creativity.

No doubt integrating inner harmonies with outer obligations would be a real challenge and on a continuing basis. Would dreamwork be able to overcome the rational orthodoxy by questioning the masculine model of executive development? After defying the stereotype, would this initiative be able to survive? Apparently it has. To tell you the story.

Dreaming across cultures

On my return to India, I received a message from Dr von Franz for the 'Dreaming in India' conference together with an unexpected gift: an enlightening story from the *Brihadaranya Upanishad* (literally, the secret doctrine taught in the large forest) meant to indicate the method of receiving instruction and is particularly an eulogy on knowledge (see Appendix 3). It was strange that this story embodying age-old wisdom had come to me from Switzerland.

For me, this marked the beginning of a new era; an era where the cultural heritage of one civilization will be available to the entire global family. In fact, a great cultural shift is taking place as the boundaries between East and West are gradually getting blurred. Will this lead to a synthesis of cultures across the globe?

'Can our dreams lead us to better understand culture?' 'Can we learn to look at dreams from this perspective?' These were the questions asked by one of the participants of the dreaming in India' conference held in Pune in January 1995. This conference brought together people from the United States, France, Germany, Holland, Japan, South Korea and India.

The following is the dream of a Japanese sand-play therapist in which she comes to terms with herself and an important aspect of a relationship in which culture plays a dominant role.

I am embarrassed to find myself in a strange room upon awakening. What will my roommate at the Conference think? When I walk back to the original room I am surprised to find that the room does not have a regular wooden door but a broken shoji,a partition made with bamboo sticks. This reminds me of my in-laws' room in our home in Tokyo.

Then the scene shifts to back home. On my way to the bedroom I peep into my in-laws' room. They are not yet asleep. I hope that they have not noticed that I am drunk. I experience a sense of embarrassment and relief.

By the time the dreamer completed the description of the broken shoji—a paper screen with thin walls that are easy to move, and peer through—she could see the link between the broken shoji and her dysfunctional relationship with her mother-in-law. She had always found it difficult to relate to her mother-in-law as if an invisible partition existed between them. This issue had been a source of constant embarrassment and frustration to her because as a therapist she expected to excel in every relationship.

While working on the dream a forgotten incident flashed back. In an office party long ago she had got so upset by a remark of the head of the institute that she had splashed whisky on his face in anger. This incident had brought her face to face with an unpleasant aspect of herself: her intolerant and defensive attitude. It was antithetical to a culture which emphasizes the collective, and where authority, age and position are greatly respected and greater tolerance towards others is expected. The acute sense of embarrassment and the deep anguish it caused became a doorway through which her own developmental journey began.

The broken shoji in the dream evoked multidimensional associations for the dreamer. But one image in particular opened up the dream to the dreamer. She stated that she herself felt like a broken shoji, in dire need of rectifying her defensive nature. She further stated that the broken shoji in many ways reflected that the Japanese culture was fading and thus urgently in need of revival. She became acutely conscious of this cultural dimension only during the process of sharing the dream at the conference.

The Japanese culture like many others around the world is in transition, in a process of renaissance and transformation. While the dream of an individual reflects culture, it also offers a critique of culture and a realm of relative freedom and transformation.

In that sense, dreams and dreamwork can safely be regarded as ways of coping with our own existential dramas. For example, one of the participants of 'Dreaming in Russia' in 1991 acknowledged that although he had been engulfed by a certain darkness over that summer, he had discovered that his own personal cataclysm melted into the greater socio-historical cataclysm providing a great release as well as a genuine concern for issues more global (Dupre 1992). It seems that although we are aware of the familiar causes of human anguish, the cultural component carries as equal weight, for we are all products of our own cultures.

The inner conditions of the self therefore often resonate with the outer conditions. It is not unusual for individual dreams to reflect the turmoil of the collective society. The I Ching has already shown us that 'if the myth is the outer expression of the human conditions, basic struggles, joys and ambiguities, then the dream is its inner voice'.

In that multicultural, multilingual group, dreamwork taught us acceptance and tolerance; tolerance of the diverse ways of viewing culture and an understanding of diverse lifestyles.

Dreamwork often enhances our capacity to empathize with different aspects of the self, to encounter different voices within ourselves and to integrate conflictual aspects of the self.

When we encounter the conflicting aspects within ourselves, we also begin to be more tolerant of others. The awareness of the multiplicity of the self and identification with diverse aspects of ourselves in dreamwork enhances our ability to empathize with others while awake. This learning can help us develop resilience to the complexities and ambiguities of contemporary times and, in the process, lead us to a sense of belonging—the realization that despite surface differences, we belong to life; to each other, and to Nature.

Similar feelings were echoed by a practising lawyer of the Supreme Court of India who attended the 'Dreaming in India' conference. Dreams provide an effective channel to express the suppressed emotions of the day. However, if ignored, these emotions often erupt without any warning and get acted upon on people around us. As I have often observed, whatever we deny durine the day asserts itself in dreams. Similarly, whatever is ignored or devalued by the waking consciousness emerges in dreams.

Dream images are derived from our social heritage and our current realities and it is true that not only do we reflect our culture but our culture too reflects us. No wonder dreamwork often provides a better perspective of specific dimensions of culture. This is so because we are capable of creating culture and also capable of being created by it.

The notion of interdependence, of mutual interpenetration of the self and the world opens up a possibility of wider sharing. That is exactly what Richard Russo, an American delegate and a board member of the International Association for the Study of Dreams, experienced while working on a dream of an Indian R&D manager of a petrochemicals company in the small groups. The dream deals with the chronically unresolved issue of equal division of ancestral property—a residential house and farm-land—of the dreamer's grandfather between his father and uncle.

> *At the bank of the river, there are a number of people engaged in disposing of a dead body. I am surprised to see my mother taking an active part in the process. This is simply not done. She is trying hard to push the body into the river with a bamboo stick. The body bobs up and down several times. Once it comes up with such force that my mother gets thrown off balance and falls into the river. Now it is she who is struggling for survival. There is a great deal of screaming and shouting. Ultimately, the people tie a heavy stone around the body, which finally sinks in the water.*

While sharing the dream and the context in which the dream occurred, many features of Indian culture and lifestyle were automatically highlighted. For example, women normally do not participate in the final rites of the dead, and neither do they have much say in property matters, etc. The aspects regarding Hindu traditions and burial which emerged through personal experience along with a great deal of emotion evoked empathy in others and made it possible for them to relate them with their own personal experiences and feelings.

No wonder Richard Russo commented in a letter that:

When discussing the values and beliefs of other cultures the tendency is always to perceive how different they are from our own. When sharing deep personal experiences we move towards empathy and perceiving the ways in which we are alike.

The spontaneous moments of identification with others allows one to step out of one's social identity and role. I learned more about the Indian culture and way of life than I could possibly have done any other way in so short a time (all of three weeks of stay) because everything I learnt through dream sharing was concrete and personal.

Dreams, then, do both. They reflect and transcend culture. In Russo's words I see early signs of the emergence of a new culture. As Jean Houston says: 'We are experiencing the harvest of all world's cultures, belief systems and symbolic knowing.' It centres around self-integration and connection with others around the globe: a synthesis of diverse cultures and traditions integrating the philosophies of the East and the West.

And the twain shall meet

From the Netherlands came a dreamer on a 'pilgrimage' to India in search of a mystical experience like so many before her had come. For her, as for many in the West, India is neither geography, nor political history; rather, it symbolizes an inner quest. It has therefore to be seen on the spiritual world map.

I met her in New Delhi during the International Sufi Seminar at the *dargah* (memorial tomb) of Hazrat Inayat, the great Sufi master, musician and mystic. This ordinary meeting later turned into an extraordinary one as it shone with inner significance and meaning.

'I have a dream,' she had said with a sense of urgency. 'Can I come and see you?'

A feminist and pensioner in her mid-sixties from Holland, the dreamer had decided to dedicate her life to a spiritual centre in the Netherlands. Before commencing her work at the centre, she took what she called the 'once-in-a-life-time trip' to India, now her new-found spiritual home. India represented for her ancient wisdom and liberation. Yet it fascinated her and frightened her at the same time, somewhat like her decision to dedicate her life to a 'higher purpose'.

I see a little white snake with a bright shining head in my otherwise bare hotel room. I take this little white snake to a big white snake lying on top of a cupboard. There is a Western woman in the room who seems to have easy contact with the snake. I inquire whether the big snake frightens her. She says, 'I love snakes. My whole life is devoted to looking after them.' I then wonder whether the big snake will accept my little one and whether to leave it here or to take it to a pet shop.

So I stand on a chair in order to talk to the snake lying on the cupboard. The big snake flashes a smile and says, 'You can entrust your little snake to me.' I am ecstatic. I then place my little snake on the cupboard. The big snake lovingly coils itself around the little one.

'It feels so terrific to be completely accepted or loved,' she says after a brief pause. I see her in the grip of a powerful oceanic feeling, which crashes like a wave on my shore.

'Tell me about the little white snake in the dream. How is it different from the regular black one? Is it an indication of something unusual, rare or precious?' I ask her.

'Oh, that white snake! It is the transformed version of the black snake that was once in me.' A powerful association falls into place.

As I pondered over the metaphor of a black snake, a dark shadow flitted across her face. The floodgates began to open.

'I had a lonely childhood. Often felt like nobody's child. Unloved, uncared for. During my adolescent years I began to feel like an underworld creature. Lonely, fearful and depressed. I was very suspicious of people. Any contact with them frightened me. Those years of psychiatric treatment were like living in a black hole . . . frightening . . . forbidding.' She let herself slide back into it once again, down and down she went.

I was frightened of losing her. Violent sobs racked her frail body. A window opened into that dark period in her life. It was only then that I realized the extent to which the black hole must have set limits and choked her very existence . . .

'It must have been tremendously difficult to step out of the black hole,' I said, fully in tune with her agony, pouring all my warmth and comfort in an effort to pull her out of the black hole whose mouth was rapidly closing over her. Perhaps spiritual deepening is possible only at the cost of great pain.

'Yes it was! But thank God, it's all over,' she said after a pause that felt like an eternity. 'In retrospect, I think it had something also to do with the work I did with the women's group on issues of identity. I do not know when exactly the process of asking "Who are you?" of others turned into a searching and soulsearching "Who am I?" for me. I lived with it for days on end and then something beautiful happened. I had a powerful vision. I imagined that I stood under a shower of falling stars that filled up the black hole, closing it once and for all. The vision was so powerful that I would think about it day and night. It had a transforming, strange healing quality. It changed my life completely. I began to feel whole. The snake had finally shed its black skin and with that began the process of renewal.' There was a light in her eyes as she continued, speaking with deep conviction.

'I then slowly began to recognize this new feeling that circulated within my entire body. This feeling knew no boundaries, no limits. It simply connected me to people, to the entire world. I know it sounds incredible but it is true. It has become even more pronounced during this trip to India.'

I reflected on the *kundalini*—the Indian term for the energy of the 'coiled one' sleeping at the base of the spine, waiting to be awakened. I was struck by a sense of delicate mystery here. The transformation of the raw underworld snake-consciousness to a super human consciousness, had also in the process transformed the snake poison into a healing potion.

'The dream is so special that I cannot resist telling it to people,' the dreamer said.

The memory of our first meeting flashed back. It was during the Sufi Seminar that a reference had been made to my work on dreams by one of the speakers. As a result, a few people had come up to me during the break. 'I believe you work on dreams. Have you met Ms _____ from Holland? She had a very powerful dream, you know.'

So, I had actually heard about the 'big dream' even before I had met the dreamer.

'How do you feel about the dream now?' I asked her.

'I do not know what the dream has done to me. But despite continuous travelling in a seemingly unfamiliar country, I feel younger, energetic, and completely regenerated. As if I am connected to a dynamo with an infinite supply of energy. For some strange reason I feel deeply accepted and completely at home.

'I suppose this has something to do with India, and the very special atmosphere over here,' she says, reflecting on her experience. 'India for me is the big white snake which accepts and nurtures the little white snakes. India is ancient, buried in the coils of time, yet with a presence that is immediate. She is of this world and beyond. Although India is changing, she remains unchanged in the eternal sense. It is here I receive the message of spiritual liberation—liberation from the dark forces. It is here I finally begin to feel comfortable about dedicating my life to the spiritual centre back home.'

I wondered whether leaving home is necessary in order to find our innermost core. Perhaps one does not consciously decide to leave home. It just happens. As Anderson and Hopkins (1992) say, it does not necessarily mean that you leave anything or anybody.

> What is left or lost is not a relationship or a place or even a context. What is left is a consciousness that once felt secure and what replaces this sureness is a state of not knowing. An openness. Sometimes home-leaving can help widen or deepen a track already running silently in one's life. To let go of all preconceptions and expectations, to let go of desire, to be in control—as often happens—in a foreign country or a strange territory and to be open to what is actually happening, is like accepting life at a much deeper level.

This, of course, is what dreamwork is all about. In the final analysis, we are healed of what we turn towards and not what we turn away from. By working on dreams and sharing them in a spirit of receptivity and reciprocity, two opposite poles merge and become one. One seeks a spiritual message of deliverance in the East through a dream incubated in the Oriental soil. The other finds a keynote of her soul during her brief sojourn in the Western land of dreams.

And when I take a deep look within myself I discover that the East and the West can actually meet within me at that special junction which lies between dreaming and waking.

After all, 'In a circle, the points of the beginning and the end are the same.'

General Questions About Dreams

Does everyone dream?

Yes. Research over the last four decades has shown that every human being has regular periods throughout the night during which dreaming takes place.

Why do people have difficulty remembering their dreams?

Dream recall differs from person to person. Research indicates that some people recall their dreams very vividly, others only occasionally, while some others believe that they are non-dreamers. Generally speaking, most dreams are forgotten unless they are written down. Sometimes a fragment of a dream is suddenly remembered later in the day or even days later, suggesting that the memory is triggered by an incident in the waking state and that it is not entirely lost but for some reason very difficult to retrieve. Sleep and dreams are also affected by fatigue, drugs, medication and alcohol.

Do we dream in colour or black and white?

Most dreams are in colour because colour is a natural part of our visual experience. However, there are people who report dreaming in black and white. Everything in dreams including colour is significant for deriving meaning.

What is a recurring dream, or why do we have the same dream over and over again?

A recurring dream is spurred by incidents, thoughts and feelings that remind the dreamer of an unresolved issue of the past.

Understanding the meaning of such dreams can sometimes help resolve an issue that the dreamer has been struggling with for years.

A dream experience is a subjective, personal experience. How do we know it is authentic?

It is true that a dream experience is inherently subjective, a personal viewpoint and a personal perspective. What is important to remember here is that it is not *the* experience or *the best* experience but *an* experience that makes sense from a certain perspective. For example, research has established the effectiveness of painkillers in spite of the fact that pain is a personal, subjective experience.

Hence, it can be stated that privately experienced things can be made public to the extent that they are a part of our shared reality.

Much of subjective experience does not appear to fit into the accepted scientific viewpoint. How can we integrate the insights derived through dreamwork into business management?

There is a common belief that science describes reality on the basis of the data received only from the senses, that is, from experiences of the physical world, but does not take into account the broad spectrum of inner realities—the vast range of experiences of conscious awareness, intentionality, memory, volition, aesthetic sense, which describe the other aspects of reality. One of the things dreamworking teaches us is that we need to acknowledge the existence of multiple interpretations of reality.

Recalling and understanding our dreams requires effort. Does that mean that we will be deprived of the much-needed rest at night?

Studies have shown that dreams are not only psychologically meaningful but even physiologically so. It is on account of their physiological importance that each one of us dreams every night, irrespective of recall. Actually, when we sleep our brains continue to function, like computers during off-line processing. They 'tidy' up memory, merge new experiences with the old, discard outdated information, relabel and integrate files. In short, while we sleep the brain just switches from the verbal to the visual. Dreams continue the work begun during waking life, although we are unaware of this. For instance, it is a common experience that when we sleep on a problem it gets sorted out, and when we awaken the next morning the solution is clear to us. All that we do through dreamwork is create an awareness of this fact and explore ways and means of harnessing the innate problem-solving function of our sleeping mind.

Is it dangerous to work on dreams?

Dreams have for long remained shrouded in mystery. They have been associated with parapsychology, the occult and the supernatural. Until Freud's *Interpretation of Dreams* there had been no truly scientific approach to the understanding of dreams. However, the discovery of the cyclic nature of sleep in 1952 exploded many long-held myths about dreams and also replaced fantasy with fact.

As a result, 'dreaming' as a subject has come within the purview of scientific study, which has demystified dreams. Moreover, contemporary dreamwork has established that a dream is the product of a dreamer's thoughts, feelings and experiences—a resource to be harnessed, not ignored or be frightened of.

What can often cause discomfort is the fact that dreams hold a mirror in front of us and what we see reflected in it might not be very flattering. It can force us to take a harder look at ourselves and face up to the fact that we have anxieties and hostilities that we do not want to accept, even to ourselves. It can leave us feeling that we were better off without this new piece of information. This has been a classical attitude whenever anything new is incorporated in the already existing body of knowledge. On the other hand, dreams often also reveal the hidden talents, unused creative potential and ideas we never credited ourselves with.

How can we improve our work-related skills (technical skills) with dreamwork?

This can be best answered by a story. A human factors' expert was once asked: 'How do you build a frog? Do you study the croak, the famous "leap" or the hyperbolic eyes?' 'No,' the expert said, 'you study the pond.' The environment or the pond will give a clue to the frog you have been asked to build.

So is the case with dreams. A dream is an environment where an actually lived life really unfolds. Future managers are expected to excel in an environment which is continually being shaped and reshaped by change. This change alters not only the essence of business but also the nature of the skills necessary to govern it.

If this analogy is applied to organizational systems, then it is the environment that encourages people to explore new ideas and take meaningful risks at reasonable costs. Hence, the most successful innovation systems are environments, where curiosity is as much valued as any other technical skill.

My study with hundreds of managers from diverse sectors of business as also the work done with several other professionals indicates that dreamwork can be imparted as a training in executives' education as it provides an opportunity for learning new skills and enhancing creative potential.

The only learning that significantly influences behaviour is self-discovered learning. Dreamwork provides a chance for such learning that leads to the development of greater flexibility, adaptability and a broader behavioural repertoire which enables managers to function in a variety of situations.

APPENDIX 2

Dream Interviewer's Cue Card*

Questions you can ask yourself, or a client, or friend to explore the meaning of a dream.

You may find the dreamer better able to answer your questions if you first ask him to pretend that you come from another planet. This way, when you ask him, 'Who is Bob Hope?' he won't simply answer, 'You know who Bob Hope is!' and miss the opportunity of discovering his own specific associations to the man. So often, what a dreamer assumes to be general knowledge or fact about a given figure or event is really a very personal web of attitudes, beliefs and associations. Furthermore, the words the dreamer uses to describe a dream image will be the best ones to repeat to him in order to trigger relevant associations to his current life situation. Use the interviewer's cue card after the dreamer has told you the dream in the first person and present tense, as if he were reliving it.

Initial questions

1. When you re-experience the feelings you had in the dream, do they remind you of anything in your current life?

2. Describe the opening setting of the dream: place, mood, feelings.

3. Does this remind you of anything? Does the location, mood, or do these feelings remind you of a situation in your life? Ask this about each setting in the dream.

* Reproduced with permission from Gayle Delaney, *Living Your Dreams*, Harper & Row, 1981. © 1984 Gayle Delaney. All rights reserved.

4. Who is X? Ask the dreamer to tell you who each person in the dream is. He will respond best if you remind him that you come from another planet and do not know a thing about Earth life. If you avoid asking 'What does "X" *mean* to you,' you can bypass premature interpretive efforts and help the dreamer better explore and experience the reality of the image. Later questions should then reveal the meanings with less effort as the descriptions and definitions make correspondences to life situations evident.

5. What is X like? This will encourage the producer to tell you what he thinks of X, and he will usually supply associations automatically. Another way to phrase this question is to ask what kind of person X is. Encourage the dreamer to give you his impressions of the dream person as he is in waking life and not to worry about being accurate or objective. If X is a person unknown to the dreamer, ask, 'What kind of person would you imagine X might be like?'

6. What is X like in your dream? What is X doing in your dream? By asking this sort of question, you can find out what specific aspects of X are emphasized in a particular dream, as well as how these qualities help or hinder the dreamer.

7. Does X remind you of anything in your life? By repeating to the dreamer the descriptions he has just given you (using the same adjectives and tone) the dreamer will often be able to link the description to someone close to him, to a force in his life or to an aspect of himself. If not, you can ask:

8. Is there some part of you which is like X? You may meet with a lot of resistance here, especially if the dreamer has just described someone he strongly dislikes. While you may see some of X's characteristics in the dreamer, timing is all-important. An offended producer won't talk much. You can always return to this or any questions later when the interview has warmed up a bit.

9. What is your waking relationship with X like? With this question you are trying to discover the nature of the relationship—intimate, casual, troublesome, enriching, etc. The dreamer will often supply revealing anecdotes of the history of the relationship if given the chance or the encouragement.

10. What is a Y? Ask the producer to define each of the major objects in the dream and tell you what it is used for and how it works. Remind him that you come from another planet and have never seen nor heard of a Y. Reassure him that you are interested not in scientific accuracy but in his ideas or understanding of what a Y is and how it works. If you ask what does a *'Y' mean* to you, you usually get a premature interpretation—get a definition first.

11. What is the Y in your dream like, and what does it remind you of? When the producer describes his dream objects, he may also add some associations, which you may or may not want to explore further.

12. Describe the major action or events in the dream and tell me what they remind you of in your waking life.

With practice, a flexible use of these questions will unlock the meaning of a dream. Often you will have to follow-up with questions specific to the given dream. A fuller explanation of this dream-interviewing process will be found in Chapter 3 of Delaney's book, *Living Your Dreams.*

APPENDIX 3

The Four States of Being

Scattered throughout the religious scriptures of India, parables and stories abound, weaving a colourful thread around the most profound spiritual truths of mankind. The Upanishads speak to us of the way in which the individual self can reach the ultimate reality by an inward journey, an inner ascent. They primarily speak of four states of being in this journey towards ultimate reality—waking, dreaming, dreamless sleep, and the supernatural, transcendent, fourth state. This story, in the form of a dialogue between Janaka, king of Vaideha, and the sage Yajnavalkya, is both entertaining and enlightening.

King Janaka was a seeker of knowledge, yet he continued to be a householder and performed his worldly duties with perfect detachment. Janaka was the greatest disciple of Yajnavalkya, who made momentous contribution towards the spiritual education and uplift of his disciples.

Once, Janaka Vaideha and Yajnavalkya had a disputation on the *agnihotra* (daily offering of oblations in the sacred fire). Yajnavalkya had granted Janaka Vaideha a boon, and he chose (for a boon) that he might be free to ask him any question he liked. Yajnavalkya granted it, and thus the king was the first to ask him a question.

'Yagnavalkya,' the king said, 'what serves as the light for man? What is the true essence of man?'

Yagnavalkya replied: 'The light of the Sun, O King; for, having the sun alone for his light, he sits, moves about, does his work, and returns.'

Janaka Vaideha said: 'So indeed it is, O Yagnavalkya.'

Janaka Vaideha said: 'When the sun has set, O Yagnavalkya, what then serves as the light for man?

Yagnavalkya replied: 'The moon indeed is his light; for,

having the moon alone for his light, he sits, moves about, does his work, and returns.'

Janaka Vaideha said: 'So indeed it is, O Yagnavalkya.'

Janaka Vaideha said: 'When the sun has set, O Yagnavalkya, and the moon has set, what is the light of man?'

Yagnavalkya replied: 'The fire indeed serves as his light; for, having fire alone for his light, man sits, moves about, does his work, and returns.'

Janaka Vaideha said: 'When the sun has set, O Yagnavalkya, and the moon has set, and the fire has gone out, what is then the light of man?'

Yagnavalkya replied: 'Speech (sound) indeed is his light; for, having speech (sound) alone for his light, man sits, moves about, does his work, and returns. Therefore, O King, when one cannot see even one's own hand, yet when a sound is uttered, one manages to go towards it.'

Janaka Vaideha said: 'So indeed it is, O Yagnavalkya.

Janaka Vaideha said: 'When the sun has set, O Yagnavalkya, and the moon has set, and the fire is gone out, and the sound hushed, what serves as the light for man?'

Yagnavalkya said: 'The self indeed serves as his light, for having the self alone as his light, man sits, moves about, does his work, and returns.'

Janaka Vaideha said: 'Who is that self?'

Yagnavalkya replied: 'The self-luminous being who dwells within the lotus of the heart, surrounded by the senses and sense organs and who is the light of the intellect. Becoming identified with the intellect, he moves to and fro, through birth and death, between this world and the next. Becoming identified with the intellect, the self appears to be thinking, appears to be moving, in the two worlds of knowledge. He, remaining the same, wanders along the two worlds. In this world, while awake or dreaming; in the other world as if thinking, as if moving. During sleep (being identified with the dream) he transcends this world and all the, forms of death (all that falls under the sway of death, all that is perishable).

References and Select Bibliography

Amabile, T.M. and **S.S. Grysklewicz**, (1988), 'Creative human resources', in R.L. Kuhn (ed.), *The R&D Lab Handbook of Creative and Innovative Managers,* McGraw-Hill, New York.

Andel, P.V. (1992), 'Serendipity—Expect also the unexpected', *Creativity and Innovation Management,* Vol. I, No. 1, March.

Anderson, S.R. and **P. Hopkins** (1992), 'Leaving home', *Noetic Sciences Review,* No. 21, Spring.

Asrensky, E. and **N. Klietman** (1953), 'Regularly occurring periods of eye mobility and concomitant phenomena during sleep', *Science,* No. 118, pp. 273.

Avasthatraya, 'The three states', *Mandukya Upanishad.*

Barron, F. (1971), 'An eye more fantastical', in G. Davies and J. Scott (eds), *Training Creative Thinking,* Holt, Rinehart & Winston, New York.

Baynes, C.F. (1950), *I Ching: The Book of Changes,* Princeton University Press, Princeton, N.J.

Bohm, D. (1980), *Wholeness and Implicate Order,* Routledge & Kegan Paul, London.

Bosnak, Robert (1995), 'Experiment in social dreaming', Dreaming in India, unpublished report, Sudbury, Massachusetts.

Bower, J.L. and **C.M. Christensen** (1995), *Harvard Business Review,* Jan–Feb.

Breger, L., I. Hunter and **R.W. Lane** (1971), *The Effect of Stress on Dreams,* International University Press, New York.

Bremmerman, H. (1995), 'Self-organisation in evolution, immune systems, economics, neural nets and brains', in R.K. Mishra, D. Maab and E. Zwierein (eds), *Springer Series in Synergetics,* Vol. 61, Springer Verlag, Berlin, Heidelberg, p. 11. Also, personal correspondence and a mimeographed paper, courtesy of the author.

Cartright, R.D. (1991), 'Dreams that work: The relation of dream incorporation to adaptation to stressful events', *Dreaming,* Vol. 1, No. 1.

Delaney, G. (1981), *Living Your Dreams,* Harper & Row, New York.

Dror, Yehezkel (1968), *Public Policy Making Reexamined,* Station, Chandler, p. 49.

Drucker, P.F. (1985), *Innovation and Entrepreneurship,* Harper & Row, New York.

Dupre, Michael (1992), 'Russia dreaming liberation', *Dreaming,* Vol. II, No. 2, June.

Evans, P. and **G. Dechan** (1990), *The Keys to Creativity,* Grafton Books, London.

Fabun, D. (1970), *Three Rounds of Awareness,* Glencoe Press, Beverly Hills.

Fagin, H. (1987), 'Creativity and dreams', in M. Ullman and C. Limmer (eds), *Dream Experience,* pp. 59–79.

Freud, S. (1965), *Interpretation of Dreams,* standard edition, New York, p. 386.

Garfield, P. (1974), *Creative Dreaming,* Ballantine, New York.

———— (1991), *The Healing Power of Dreams,* Simon & Schuster, New York.

Gee, C. (1985), 'Creativity in science and the arts: Similarities are marked', a report in *Quarterly, Creativity and Innovation Network,* T. Richards (ed.), April–June, pp. 68–69.

Getzels, J.W. and **Csikszentmihalyi, M.** (1976), *The Creative Vision,* John Wiley & Sons, New York.

Goleman, B. (1996), *Emotional Intelligence,* Bantam Books, New York.

Gordon, W. (1961), *Synectics: The Development of Creative Capacity,* Collier, New York.

Gould, S.J. (1993), *Eight Little Piggies,* Penguin, London.

Hall, D.T. (1972), 'A model of coping with role conflict', *Administrative Science Quarterly,* No. 17, pp. 471–86.

Harman, W. and **H. Rheingold** (1984), *Higher Creativity,* The Putnam Berkeley Group Inc.

Hartman, E. (1991), *The Boundaries in the Mind,* Basic Books, New York.

Hazarika, A. (1994), 'Dreaming the new paradigm for change and development', in U. Kohli and D. Sinha (eds), *Human Resources Development: Global Challenges and Strategy for 2000 A.D.,* Allied Publishers, New Delhi.

———— (1995), 'Harnessing managerial potential through dreams', in F. Massarick (ed.), *Advances in Organization Development,* Vol. III, Ablex Publishing Company, New Jersey.

———— (1996), 'Stimulating business creativity through dreams', paper presented at the Annual International Conference of the Association of Dreams, Berkeley.

Houston, J. (1994), 'Calling our spirits home', *Noetic Sciences Review,* No. 32, Winter.

Hughes, T.P. (1989), *American Genesis: A Century of Invention and Technological Enthusiasm,* Viking, New York.

Jung, C.G. (1963), *Memories, Dreams and Reflections,* Random House, New York.

Koestler, A. (1964), *The Act of Creation,* Arkana, London.

Kopp S. (1976), *If You Meet the Buddha on the Road Kill Him,* Bantam Books, New York, p. 12.

Krippner, S. and **J. Dillard** (1988), *Dreamworking,* Bearly, New York.

Kuhn, R.L. (ed.) (1988), *Handbook of Creative and Innovative Managers,* McGraw-Hill, New York.

Lancourt, Joan (1996), *Leading Organization Transformation Prism,* Arthur D'Little, Third Quarter.

Mackenzie, N. (1965), *Dreams and Dreaming,* Vanguard Press Inc., New York.

Mackinnon, D.W. (1971), 'Educating for creativity—A modern myth', in G. Davies and J. Scott (eds), *Training Creative Thinking,* Holt, Rinehart & Winston, New York, p. 206.

Madhavananda, Swami (tr.) (1993), *The Brhadaranyaka Upanisad,* Advaita Ashram Publication, Calcutta.

Mandi, A. and **D. Sethi** (1996), 'Either/or yields to the theory of both', *The Times of India,* 4 April.

Mattoon, M. (1984), *Understanding Dreams,* Spring Publications, Dallas.

McAleer, N. (1989), 'On creativity', *Omni,* Vol. II, No. 7, pp. 99–102.

Mclelland, D. (1963), 'The calculated risk—An aspect of scientific performance in creativity', in C. Taylor (ed.), *Scientific Creativity: Its Recognition and Development,* John Wiley & Sons, New York, quoted in G.T. Geis (1988), 'Making companies creative', in R.L. Kuhn (ed.), *Handbook of Creative and Innovative Managers,* McGraw-Hill, New York.

Menezes, F. (1987), 'Dreamwork in organizational development at an R&D centre', paper presented at the IVth International Conference of the Association for the Study of Dreams, University of Marymount Arlington, Virginia.

———— (1992), 'The potential of dreamwork in management and personal growth training', *TMTC Journal of Management,* Vol. II, No. 1.

Mindell, A. (1982), *Dreambody: The Body's Role in Revealing the Self,* Sigmo Press, Boston, Massachusetts.

Mintzberg, H. (1976), 'Planning on the left side managing on the right', *Harvard Business Review,* July–Aug.

Newell, A. and **H. Simon** (1972), *Human Problem Solving,* Prentice Hall, Englewood Cliffs, N.J.

Newmann, E. (1959), *Art and the Creative Unconscious,* Bollingen Series XI, Princeton University Press, Princeton, N.J., pp. 193–94.

O'Flaherty (1987), *Dreams, Illusions and Other Realities,* Motilal Banarasidass, New Delhi.

Osborne, A.F. (1963), *Applied Imagination,* Charles Scriber & Sons, New York.

Parnes, S.J. (1971), 'Can creativity be increased', in G. Davies and J. Scott (eds), *Training Creative Thinking,* Holt, Rinehart & Winston, New York, pp. 64–75.

Perkins, D. (1981), *The Mind's Best Work,* Harvard University Press, Cambridge, M.A.

Perls, F.S. (1969), *Gestalt Therapy Verbatim Lafayette,* Real People Press, California, p. 67.

Poincare, H. (1924), *Foundation of Science,* tr. G.B. Halstead, Science Press, New York.

Prakash, Saurabh (1996), 'And the dreamer dreams on', unpublished manuscript.

Rawlinson, J.G. (1981), *Creative Thinking and Brainstorming,* Gower, Aidersnot.

Ray, Paul (1996), 'The rise of integral culture', *Noetic Sciences Review,* No. 37, Spring.

Repucci, L.C. (1971), 'What research reveals about creativity', in G. Davies and J. Scott (eds), *Training Creative Thinking,* Holt, Rinehart & Winston, New York, pp. 64–75.

Sacks, O. (1989), *Seeing Voices,* Pan, London.

Sattler, R. (1995), 'Life science and spirituality', lecture delivered on the occasion of the 60th birthday of His Holiness the Dalai Lama, New Delhi.

Schwartz, Felice (1990), 'Management, women and the new facts of life', *Harvard Business Review,* Autumn.

Shah, Idries (1964), *The Sufis,* Anchor Books, Doubleday, New York.

Sorokin, P.A. (1962), *Social and Cultural Dynamics,* Vol. 4, Badminister Press.

Steinem, Gloria (1992), *Revolution from Within,* Little Brown & Company, Boston.

Taub-Bynum, B.C. (1984), *The Family Unconscious,* Quest Wheaton III, Theological Publishing House, 1984.

Torrance, E.P. (1971), 'Nurture of creative talents', in G. Davies and J. Scott (eds), *Training Creative Thinking,* Holt Rinehart & Winston, New York, pp. 208–19.

———— (1972), *Guiding Creative Talent,* Prentice Hall, Englewood Cliffs, New Jersey.

Toynbee, A. (1947), *A Study of History,* abridgement of vols I–VI by D.D. Somerwell, Oxford University Press.

Ullman, M. (1987), 'The experiential dream group', in M. Ullman and C. Limmer (eds), *The Variety of Dream Experience,* Continuing Publishing Co., New York.

———— (1996), *Appreciating Dreams,* Sage Publications Inc., Thousand Oaks.

Ullman, M. and **N. Zimmerman** (1979), *Working with Dreams,* Jeremy Tarcher, Los Angeles.

Wallas, A. (1926), *The Art of Thought,* Harcourt Brace, New York.

Watkins, M. (1992), 'Perestroika of the self: Dreaming in the USSR', *Dreaming,* Vol. II, No. 2, June.

———— (1987), 'Moral imagination and peace action', in V. Andrews, R. Bosnak and K.W. Goodwin (eds), *Facing Apocalypse,* Spring Publication Inc., Texas.

Wayman A. (1984), 'Significance of dreams in India and Tibet', in A. Wayman (ed.), *Buddhist Insight,* Motilal Banarasidass, p. 405. Also, personal correspondence.

Winter, D.G. (1973), *The Power Motive,* The Free Press, New York.

Woodman, M. (1993), 'Stepping over the threshold', *Noetic Sciences Review,* No. 28, Sausalito, California.

Woodward, Nick (1995), 'Systemic changes in internal and external organisation', paper presented at the International Roundtable on Enterprise Restructuring through Systemic Change: Issues and Strategies, New Delhi.

Acknowledgements

In writing this book, I am grateful to many.

My introduction to dreamwork came from Francis Menezes. I am indebted to him for his direction, especially in the early years of my initiation to dreamwork.

I am extremely grateful to Dr Montague Ullman in more ways than one. His pioneering work has been a source of inspiration and my work has greatly benefited from its insights. I am thankful that he could spare the time to read through the manuscript and give me penetrating suggestions.

Gayle Delaney has been a friend and fellow professional and I have enjoyed every moment of our work together. I would like to thank her for her spontaneous and encouraging response to the book. I am grateful to Dr Venkataraman of Engineers India Ltd, for his words of wisdom.

All those dreamers who have gifted their dream documents to this book need special thanks. Without this gesture, their experiences with dreams could not possibly have become a learning experience for all.

I cannot thank enough Shankar Hazarika, my brother-in-law, who is Art Director at Madison Advertising for his creative conceptualization of the cover and the illustrations and for his generosity of spirit, selflessness and enthusiasm. He gave me quality time despite his ever-demanding schedule. His creative direction and Sanjay Dabholkar's artwork have enhanced the visual appeal of the book.

Ranjan Kaul of Response Books was instrumental in initiating this project. Without his active involvement and support at various stages of this project, it would not have materialized.

Thanks are due to Shyama Warner, my editor at Response; it was a pleasure to work with her. To Reena Joseph for her enthusiastic assistance on the computer.

My immediate family, Anjan, Antara, Abhishek and Ai, put up with me—physically present but mentally preoccupied—during the course of my writing this book. To them, my most heartfelt thanks for their understanding, love and unfailing support.

Anjali Hazarika

Index

About the Author

Anjali Hazarika, Ph.D., is currently the director of the National Petroleum Management Programme (NPMP), a learning network of oil industry organizations in India.

A management trainer and corporate consultant, Dr Hazarika has introduced a large number of Indian managers from a wide range of corporations to the art and practice of dreamwork. Based on her experiential work in the corporate sector, she has presented papers at various international conferences, including at the International Conference of the Association for the Study of Dreams (Chicago 1990, Santa Cruz 1992 and Berkeley 1996) and at the World Congress of the International Federation of Training and Development Organizations (1994). She was also one of the programme directors for the International Conference on Dreaming in India held in January 1995.

Dr Hazarika writes regularly in the media, delivers public lectures, and appears on television and radio talk shows to demystify dreams and restore their value and significance in contemporary life. In addition to her work on dreams, she is actively involved with women's issues in business and has written extensively on the subject. She has edited several monographs and contributed chapters to professional publications from India and abroad. Dr Hazarika is the founder Secretary of the Forum of Women in the Public Sector under the aegis of the Standing Conference of Public Enterprises (SCOPE), New Delhi.